United Nations Centre on Transnational Corporations
United Nations Conference on Trade and Development

The Impact of **Trade-related Investment Measures** on Trade and Development

Theory, Evidence and Policy Implications

United Nations New York, 1991

NOTE

The term "country" as used in this paper also refers, as appropriate, to territories or areas; the designations employed and the presentation of the material in this paper do not imply the expression of any opinion whatsoever on the part of the Secretariat of the United Nations concerning the legal status of any country, territory, city or area or of its authorities, or concerning the delimitation of its frontiers or boundaries. In addition, the designations of country groups are intended solely for statistical or analytical convenience and do not necessarily express a judgement about the stage of development reached by a particular country or area in the development process.

The following symbols have been used in the tables:

Two dots (..) indicate that data are not available or are not separately reported;

A dash (-) or zero (0) indicates that the amount is nil or negligible.

A blank in a table indicates that the item is not applicable;

A slash (/) indicates a financial year, e.g. 1988/89;

Use of a hyphen (-) between dates representing years, for example, 1985-1989, signifies the full period involved, including the beginning and end years.

Reference to "dollars" ($) means United States dollars, unless otherwise indicated.

Annual rates of growth or change, unless otherwise stated, refer to annual compound rates.

Details and percentages in tables do not necessarily add to totals because of rounding.

ST/CTC/120

UNITED NATIONS PUBLICATION

Sales No. E.91.II.A.19

ISBN 92-1-104377-8

Manufactured in the United States of America

Preface

Trade-related investment measures have been among the most contentious issues in the Uruguay Round of Multilateral Trade Negotiations under the General Agreement on Tariffs and Trade. These negotiations, launched by the Punta del Este Ministerial Declaration of 20 September 1986, did not reach agreement at the scheduled conclusion of the negotiations in December 1990. The negotiations were resumed in February 1991.

Although trade liberalization has been the major focus of the Uruguay Round negotiations, the most controversial areas of the Uruguay Round have been the so-called new issues, namely trade-related investment measures (TRIMs), trade-related aspects of intellectual property rights (TRIPs) and trade in services.

A central concern of the TRIMs debate has been the impact of national foreign-direct-investment regulations on international trade flows. Is this impact distortionary? Under what circumstances and assumptions? Do these measures enhance or reduce the economic welfare of all countries, including the countries applying them? And what is their contribution to the development process and to the control of anti-competitive practices? These and similar questions, although crucial to decision-making, could not be answered definitively in the course of the negotiations.

As part of their research and advisory work on trade, investment and development issues, the United Nations Centre on Transnational Corporations and the United Nations Conference on Trade and Development undertook to explore these questions in a comprehensive research project, with financing from the UNCTAD/UNDP Technical Assistance Programme, designed to assist developing countries to participate more effectively in the Uruguay Round. The results are presented in this technical paper.

The principal author of this study is Theodore H. Moran. A summary of the negotiating process on TRIMs was provided by the UNCTAD Secretariat (appendix A). The study was finalized by the staff of UNCTC.

New York and Geneva, December 1991

Contents

Page

Page

Page

List of tables

Page

Introduction and overview

A. Introduction

Trade-related investment measures (TRIMs) have become a subject of considerable contention in North-South economic relations. The developed market economies — with some variations on points of detail — argue that TRIMs cause distortions in patterns of trade and investment because business decisions on the part of transnational corporations come to be made on the basis of considerations other than market forces. The developing countries argue that TRIMs can be useful policy tools to promote development objectives and strengthen trade balances. Following rhetoric which was quite vivid in its denunciation of TRIMs (e.g., "trade-related performance requirements — requiring minimum local content or export levels — now constitute one of the most serious trade policy problems facing the international trading community" [1]), the developed countries, led by the United States, moved to include TRIMs in the Uruguay Round of GATT negotiations, with the objective of controlling and ultimately prohibiting them. As discussed later, the negotiations are yet to arrive at conclusions (see appendix A for a review of the negotiations).

The term "trade-related investment measure" (TRIM) is very broad. The initial discussion of TRIMs in the general literature focused mainly on two broad categories of measures: investment incentives and performance requirements. Examples of investment incentives usually cited are subsidies, investment grants and allowances, priority access to credit, tax relief and exemptions, accelerated deductions of investment capital for tax purposes, tariff protection and other forms of fiscal, financial and commercial inducements for investments. Local content, trade-balancing and export requirements are the most

---

1 The Labor-Industry Coalition for International Trade, *Performance Requirements: A study of the Incidence and Impact of Trade-Related Performance Requirements and an Analysis of International Law* (Washington, D.C., LICIT, March 1981), p. 2.

frequently cited examples of performance requirements, although a much larger number of measures has been cited in the Uruguay Round discussions.

There is no commonly accepted method of drawing a line between the various kinds of measures (in home or host countries) which may affect the location of production and the consequent flows of goods, services, technology and capital among markets, in order to determine which of these measures are "legitimate" or otherwise. The Uruguay Round discussions have produced a list of 14 TRIMs, intended not as a definitive catalogue but as illustrations of the types of measures that may warrant some form of multilateral discipline: investment incentives, local equity requirements, licensing requirements, remittance restrictions, foreign exchange restrictions, manufacturing limitations, transfer-of-technology requirements, domestic sales requirements, manufacturing requirements, product-mandating requirements, trade-balancing requirements, local content requirements, export requirements and import-substitution requirements. In response, several developing countries suggested an expansion of this list to include home-country measures and corporate practices which could be considered TRIMs to the extent that they influence patterns of trade and investment. Overall, the measures under discussion may be divided into four broad categories: incentives, performance requirements, corporate measures and home country measures (see table 1 in chapter I).

There is no agreement, however, on how, precisely, such measures actually affect firm behaviour, or what their impact is on the structure of trade and development.

The purpose of this study is to contribute to a better understanding of the role of TRIMs in trade and development. For purposes of simplification, this study limits itself to three of the most widely discussed TRIMs: local content requirements, trade-balancing requirements and export requirements, plus the broad area of investment incentives. Drawing on new evidence and new analytical techniques, this study assesses the issue of "distortion" and attempts to draw policy conclusions of mutual benefit to developed and developing countries.

B. Executive summary

1. The characteristics of trade-related investment measures

Despite the absence of consensus on what, precisely, constitutes a trade-related investment measure, three kinds of TRIMs (domestic content, export performance, and trade-balancing requirements) have received the most intensive empirical examination. A detailed review of the six principal attempts to document TRIM characteristics shows that those studies are primarily of two types: those which elicited responses from transnational corporations about subsidiaries operating under TRIMs mandates, and those which simply amassed TRIMs regulations as listed in the statutes of individual countries.

Five conclusions emerge from a close examination of the data:

- TRIM requirements tend to be concentrated in specific industries, with the automotive, chemical and petrochemical and computer/informatics industries leading the list. This is despite the fact that regulations in a large number of countries characterize TRIMs as being generally applicable to "all" industries.
- Local content TRIMs are more frequent than export TRIMs in the automotive industry, with the reverse being true in computers/informatics. In chemicals and petrochemicals, both domestic content and export-performance TRIMs are prominent.
- TRIMs exist in both developed and developing countries, but are more frequent in the latter (although implicit TRIMs may be hidden in the former via "rules of origin" indicating a requirement for domestic content).
- In contrast to the raw numbers of countries with TRIMs, the extent of investment covered by TRIM regulations is heavily weighted towards the developed world. For example, the 20 developed countries with the most extensive presence of TRIM regulations are recipients of $230 billion in foreign direct investment from the United States; the figure for the 20 developing countries with the most extensive presence of TRIM regulations is $30 billion.
- With regard to the actual application of local content or export TRIM mandates, there is wide disparity in the data between firms reporting their developing country subsidiaries as being subject to such TRIMs (approximately 2 per cent to 6 per cent of all affiliates in the most extensive surveys) and the amount of developing country investment hypothetically or nominally covered by such TRIMs (45 per cent to 62 per cent of all investment). Two possible (complementary) explanations find support in the data: first, that the majority of TRIMs on the books are in fact discretionary and negotiable, and are often not required; and second, that many TRIMs are "redundant" in the sense of simply accelerating the plans of firms to develop local suppliers and enter export markets. A second examination of 682

investment projects found that, in 83 per cent of the cases in which firms were required to accomplish TRIM objectives (local sourcing, exporting), they planned to carry out those operations anyway.

2. *Trade and developmental effects*

Trade-related investment measures are one area of economic analysis in which theoretical considerations have crucial relevance. In the neo-classical paradigm, under assumptions of perfect competition, TRIMs are clearly distortionary to patterns of trade and development. The basic argument here is that TRIMs subtract from the welfare of all nations, including the host country which imposes them. Even export-performance TRIMs are deemed likely to worsen rather than improve the host country's trade balance. There is thus little wonder that most economists condemn them. Moreover, since TRIMs may produce abrupt shifts in firm behaviour under competitive conditions, the world trading community has an interest in proscribing them (if these assumptions are correct).

In contrast, in recent investigations associated with strategic trade theory, assumptions about perfect competition are relaxed. Under conditions of oligopoly in the industries in which international investment takes place, public policy interventions can shift rents and producer surplus to countries where the investment is located. When there are increasing returns to scale and dynamic gains from learning, strategic trade theory shows that the distribution of international production and trade is much less "given" than traditional trade theory suggests, with public policy-driven scale economy specialization overlaying a comparative advantage base. In industries with multiple operating sites of roughly comparable end-of-learning-curve costs (and/or where the cost of finding the optimal site is high in comparison to the operating cost differential), activist hosts win out. States which misconstrue the industries as having neo-classical properties, in contrast, and wait passively for markets to work on their own, lose.

Drawing on a simple model from Paul Krugman to illustrate a public policy perspective for oligopolistic industries with increasing returns to scale (see appendix B), it is demonstrated formally that there is a substantial dimension of rent-and-producer surplus (gains for infra-marginal workers and suppliers) which any given host and all other potential hosts have an interest in procuring for themselves. To pursue a development strategy to capture this rent-and-producer surplus, domestic content and export-performance TRIMs are probably not the first-best tools. However, an approach using TRIMs may have special advantages when dealing with international investors with high exit costs in the home country (including the opposition of organized labour), a preference for risk-aversion and rigidities in altering established patterns of intra-firm trade.

One must, however, be careful not to confuse this cautious appraisal of the use of TRIMs as policy tools as an endorsement of trade protectionism. As Jagdish Bhagwati has pointed out, even in industries with relatively few large players, trade liberalization is one of the most effective methods of stimulating competition; trade protection, in contrast, is likely to solidify non-competitive behaviour.[2] David Richardson has documented the fact that constraints on trade under conditions of imperfect competition lead to losses in efficiency two-to-three times as high as under perfect competition.[3] As a general proposition, therefore, trade liberalization still makes good sense. Under the broad rubric of allowing markets to work more effectively, it requires an empirical investigation to ascertain the conditions under with TRIMs may have a beneficial impact (or otherwise) on the welfare of host countries and on global welfare.

Turning from theory to evidence, three layers of data are examined, these being on industry structure, on firm responses to TRIMs and on the economic impact of TRIM requirements. After noting that all the principal explanations for foreign direct investment (Hymer, Kindleberger, Vernon, Caves, Williamson, and others) depend on the presence of imperfect competition, the actual examination of the structure of industries in which foreign direct investment takes place confirms the existence of high concentration ratios both in the home countries where it originates and in the host countries where it terminates. The United States, the United Kingdom, France and Germany, for example, exhibit a significant correlation between degree of oligopoly and outward investment; Brazil, Mexico and other host countries have more than 80 per cent of direct capital inflows in industries in which the four-firm concentration ratio is higher than 50 per cent. As a result, there is simply no empirical support for using the neo-classical paradigm to characterize industry structure in areas in which foreign direct investment predominates. This conclusion introduces the possibility that transnational corporations will have a choice about the location of production, the selection of inputs and the marketing of outputs which would be absent under perfectly competitive conditions; this is consistent with evidence of "stickiness" in disrupting intra-firm relations among fixed facilities. The magnitude of the stickiness

---

2 Jagdish Bhagwati, *Protectionism* (Cambridge, Mass., The MIT Press, 1988).

3 J. David Richardson, "Empirical research on trade liberalization with imperfect competition: a survey", *OECD Economic Studies*, 12 (Spring 1989), pp. 8-50.

problem should not be underestimated, since intra-firm trade ranges from one quarter to three quarters of all manufactured exports from developing countries.

The data on firm responses to TRIMs come from four detailed studies which asked how corporate behaviour would change if TRIM investment packages (including, in many cases, trade protection) were eliminated. This methodology would tend to exaggerate firm responses (and overstate the importance of TRIMs in altering trade patterns) since firms were invited to recalculate their activities in the absence of TRIMs while all other policy interventions on the part of non-TRIMs-using Governments remained in place. But all four studies reported that changes in international corporate operations attributable to TRIM requirements were relatively small. Transnational corporate investors were not significantly influenced by TRIMs in their decisions, as argued by those concerned that those measures might pose a threat to the stability of the international trading system. In light of this finding, the contention that TRIMs constitute a high priority trade policy issue does not seem to be fully supported by the data.

At the margin, however, there are consistent reports of competition among potential host countries, especially in footloose industries (with "footloose" referring to the multiple-comparable-cost site phenomenon encountered earlier). In this competition among would-be host countries, firms reported that developed countries used investment incentives with much the same effect as developing countries used TRIMs (cash grants in Ireland for operations larger than the Irish market having the same impact as export performance TRIMs were cited in several instances).

Finally, as indicated earlier, transnational corporations reported that TRIMs often merely required them to undertake operations they planned to do anyway. The TRIMs speeded their decisions, for instance, to develop local supplier networks or to launch exports.

Focusing on the economic impact of TRIMs on the allocation of resources, there is a noticeable lack of careful case studies at the micro level. Looking at what evidence is available in three industries (automotive, petrochemical and computer/informatics), one finds two distinct outcomes. On the one hand, TRIM failures, in all three industries, were associated with sub-economic size of operation, subsidies to compensate investors for high-cost operations and shelter from competition. On the other hand, TRIM successes, again in all three industries, were associated with economic size (full utilization of economies of scale), subsidies aimed at facilitating corporate exit and adjustment and at compensating for initial risk and uncertainty, and subsequent exposure to competition in world markets. The divergent outcomes support the view that TRIMs, like other public sector interventions in imperfect markets, enhance resource allocation if they help all potentially comparable locales utilize foreign investment to penetrate global markets but detract if they merely insulate high cost operations from competition.

3. *Policy implications*

It must be reiterated that one's judgement on the use of TRIMs as a tool for development or trade policy depends centrally on one's assumptions about industry structure. In this context, the policy debate over TRIMs has lagged considerably behind advances in theory and evidence associated with the management of imperfectly competitive industries. As Dani Rodrik comments:

> the new literature is a frustrating reminder to the South that too often ideas become intellectually respectable only when they become congruent with the interests of major Northern countries. Hence it is more than a little ironic that the new trade theory has developed against the backdrop of trade conflicts among developed countries, and between the United States and Japan, in particular. Market imperfections of the sort analyzed in this context would appear to be, if anything, more serious in the developing countries. Yet the new insights have still to penetrate the vast literature on trade policy in developing countries. [4]

There is, first, an analysis of TRIMs as a tool to promote economic development. For domestic content TRIMs, the greatest potential benefit resides in situations where foreign subsidiaries producing final products exercise monopsonistic power to drive down the price received by competitive domestic input suppliers, with consequent underconsumption of local components. A local content TRIM can compensate for foreign monopsonistic-induced distortion, increasing host country economic welfare. There are substantial complications, however, in trying to match a domestic content TRIM policy to situations which diverge from the highly stylized ideal usage. Any endorsement of domestic content TRIMs carries the threat that there could be a "contagion" of usage for import substitution reasons, which would hinder development efforts. Perhaps, as one analyst has quipped, that danger should

4 Dani Rodrik, "Imperfect competition, scale economies and trade policy in developing countries", in Robert E. Baldwin, ed., *Trade Policy Issues and Empirical Analysis* (Chicago, University of Chicago Press, 1988), pp. 109-110.

lead the TRIM option to be stamped "'classified' as 'for economists eyes only' until we have time to assess the full implications".[5] But obscurantism can hardly be justified as a substitute for open debate. The overall conclusion here is that development strategists will want to exercise considerable wariness in advocating even carefully circumscribed uses of domestic content TRIMs.

Export-performance TRIMs (including trade-balancing requirements), in contrast, offer a broader array of development benefits if they serve to "fix" world scale production within a host country's jurisdiction for an industry with increasing returns to scale. The result may be not only a shift of rents-cum-producer-surplus to the host economy but also, following the analysis of Elhanan Helpman and Paul Krugman in the strategic trade literature, the creation of "industrial complexes" with forward and backward linkages in non-traded intermediate goods which also enjoy increasing returns to scale. (Quite apart from the strategic trade argument, an export TRIM can also compensate for trade restrictions which discriminate against processed products, such as plywood, thereby improving the international allocation of resources.)

To obtain development benefits, an export-performance TRIM is not as efficient as a straightforward production subsidy: a production subsidy collects the inducement fee paid to the firm from taxpayers at large; an export-performance TRIM (offering access to a protected market, for example, in return for a target amount of exports) collects the inducement fee solely from local consumers of the product.

The fundamental question remains: why would a development strategist recommend an export TRIM? The answer depends upon whether the granting of production subsidies to foreign investors (running at \$100-\$300 million per plant, in some examples) is economically feasible and politically acceptable. In addition, the explicit *quid pro quo* associated with a TRIM may carry economic and political advantages (such as defusing domestic criticism which might accompany a large on-budget subsidy to a foreign firm). The shock value of threat-of-loss (of access to a protected market) with promise-of-gain (from exporting from a world-scale-sized facility) may help overcome intra-firm rigidities and risk aversion. Finally, in the arena of negotiating tactics, a list of TRIM requirements on the books may permit a host authority to act as a discriminating monopolist, offering a concession on an obligation of relatively high distaste to a foreign firm in return for a commitment of relatively high desirability to the country. Overall, however, export-performance TRIMs

---

5 Beth V. Yarbrough, "Comment", in Baldwin, ed., op. cit., p. 171.

remain a second-best development tool in the second-best world of imperfectly competitive foreign investors.

With regard to trade policy, the debate about whether TRIMs are distortionary is more complicated than conventional wisdom suggests. With developed and developing countries vying to establish world-scale production facilities on their territories, to single out one kind of locational policy while leaving all other locational policies in place would itself be distortionary. What is needed instead is a more balanced approach incorporating all locational policies affecting transnational investment patterns.

To reinforce this point, a technical evaluation of the comparability of alternative forms of public intervention on investor profitability was undertaken when the investor compares one site with another. Using new analysis by Stephen Guisinger (see appendix C), the interchangeable relationship between effective rates of protection (the incentive associated with TRIMs) and fiscal incentives (which affect the "rental cost of capital" or the "marginal effective rate of taxation") are examined. Besides demonstrating the comparability between TRIM investment packages and measures such as cash grants or tax breaks, the analysis reveals the substantial dimensions of locational inducements currently offered by European and United States state governments to attract (for example) automobile, petrochemical and computer facilities. European Governments offer cash grants up to 60 per cent of the cost of the entire investment; state governments in the United States have given as much as $325 million per project (or $108,000 per job) to foreign firms. While no explicit domestic content or export-performance regulations are involved, it would be disingenuous to argue that such efforts were not trade-related investment measures. The Federal Reserve Bank of St. Louis found a positive statistical correlation between the expenditures of individual states in the United States on investment promotion, on the one hand, and exports from those states, on the other. No less real is the import-substitution dimension of such policies among the developed nations. The trend, moreover, is worrisome. Average state expenditures in the United States to induce inward investment and to promote exports have grown over the past decade by more than 600 per cent. In the European Community, some members, led by Germany (which has traditionally urged a cap on locational incentives), are considering an expansion of regional inducements to the eastern part of the country, Poland, Hungary and Czechoslovakia.

In the Uruguay Round, the negotiations have focused on efforts to control, reduce and prohibit TRIMs. This effort is hardly consistent with a more broadly needed balanced approach to locational incentives. In seeking to proscribe the kind of investment packages most compatible with developing-country circumstances while leaving equivalent investment packages of the developed world intact, the Uruguay Round TRIMs effort could also be regarded, in itself, as distortionary. Moreover, even on its own terms, the effort could be counterproductive if it simply moved conditional incentive packets from published regulations to negotiations behind closed doors. More beneficial would be an attempt to achieve a multilateral agreement to limit all locational incentives, perhaps as part of an expanded subsidies code. An additional, and even more comprehensive, option would be the establishment of a multilateral framework of norms and standards on foreign direct investment, which would doubtless be a stabilizing force in the dynamic but volatile area of investor-government relations. The result could be a mutually advantageous ceasefire in the drift towards investment wars, in which TRIMs today play only a minor part.

I. Characteristics of trade-related investment measures

A. Overview

This chapter provides a description of TRIMs in developed and developing countries. It asks: which countries use TRIMs? What kind of TRIMs are they? Which industries are TRIMs directed towards? How do individual countries differ in their use of TRIMs? How extensive is their coverage in individual countries? From the beginning, however, three caveats are in order. These caveats anticipate extensive analytical discussions in later chapters.

- *Use of the term TRIM*. There is no commonly accepted definition of what constitutes a TRIM. Various GATT participants have introduced various definitions, yielding altogether a list of 14 measures. These include: investment incentives, local equity requirements, licensing requirements, remittance restrictions, foreign exchange restrictions, manufacturing limitations, transfer-of-technology requirements, domestic sales requirements, manufacturing requirements, product-mandating requirements, trade-balancing requirements, local content requirements, export requirements and import-substitution requirements. Several GATT participants have also suggested the addition of home-country and corporate measures that may affect trade and investment flows. The types of measures contemplated are listed in table 1.

  There is no consensus on how to determine exactly what kinds of measures should be included in discussions of policies that affect patterns of trade and production. In part, this is because the term TRIM itself appears to prejudge the question of what impact a particular measure may have in practice. In part, it is also because the term TRIM carries with it an implicitly pejorative connotation connected with the "distortion" of markets. As subsequent analysis will make clear, both the extent of impact and the issue of distortion are highly problematic.

Table 1. Trade-related investment measures and their possible impact on trade and investment

Measures	*Possible economic impact*
Investment incentives a/	Influence location of investments
Tax concessions	
Tariff concessions	
Subsidies	
Investment grants	
Performance requirements	
Local equity requirements a/	Restrict ownership of investments
Licensing requirements a/	Require technology transfer
Remittance restrictions a/	Restrict external financial transfers
Foreign exchange restrictions b/	Restrict external financial transfers
Manufacturing limitations b/	Restrict production
Transfer-of-technology requirements c/	Require technology transfer
Domestic sales requirements d/	Displace imports
Manufacturing requirements e/	Displace imports
Product-mandating requirements e/	Displace other exports
Trade-balancing requirements e/	Displace other exports
Local content requirements f/	Displace imports
Export requirements f/	Displace other imports
Import-substitution requirements	Displace imports
Corporate measures (restrictive business practices) g/	
Market allocation	Restrict exports
Collusive tendering	Excessive pricing for imports
Refusal to deal	Restrict exports/imports
Exclusive dealing	Export prohibition
Tied sales	Displace other imports/exports
Resale-price maintenance	Excessive pricing for imports
Price fixing	Excessive pricing
Differential pricing	Excessive pricing
Transfer pricing	Excessive pricing for imports; low pricing for exports
Home-country measures	
Export limitation on foreign affiliates	Restrict trade
Preferential taxes for income on investments	Subsidize investments

Source: United Nations Centre on Transnational Corporations, based on negotiating proposals in the Uruguay Round and other material.

Note: The countries identifying particular measures in the Uruguay Round are indicated as follows:

a/ United States.
b/ European Community and the United States.
c/ Japan and the United States.
d/ European Community, Japan and the United States.
e/ European Community, Japan, Switzerland and the United States.
f/ European Community, Japan, Switzerland, the Nordic countries and the United States.
g/ India.

The current study continues the practice of using the word TRIM only because all the sources of evidence employ it, and to invent a new term would be cumbersome and confusing. To show the relevance of new forms of analysis (especially strategic trade theory) for the TRIMs debate, this study will focus on local content requirements, export requirements, trade-balancing requirements and investment incentives.

- *Quality of the data.* The descriptive evidence of TRIM characteristics is scattered and of varying quality. There is no international agency with responsibility to collect and publish standardized data on TRIMs. Much of the evidence comes from interested parties in the debate about whether TRIMs constitute an appropriate tool of development or trade policy. Finally, as will become evident, one must make a careful distinction between the existence of TRIM requirements in the statutes of various countries, the exercise of TRIM requirements as part of transnational firm behaviour and the impact of TRIM requirements in changing the behaviour of transnational corporations from what it might otherwise be.
- *Evaluation of findings over time.* As will become apparent, there is no consistency of methodology over time or, for that matter, a consistency of effort. Since TRIMs are contentious, the thoroughness of the investigation may have an element of bias. The most recent data, for example, suggest the most extensive presence of TRIMs ever found; they were gathered by the Office of the United States Trade Representative, however, to help in the attempt to proscribe TRIMs in the Uruguay Round negotiations. One cannot infer, for example, that the presence of TRIMs is growing, let alone that their actual impact is rising, simply because the reporting of their existence on the books is more complete in one study than in another.

This chapter reports the findings on TRIM characteristics in section B. Section C draws conclusions from the evidence.

B. Characteristics

There have been seven major empirical attempts to gather information about TRIM characteristics, including the literature survey conducted for this study. The methodologies differ primarily in terms of whether they solicit responses from transnational firms about subsidiaries operating under TRIM requirements or whether they simply catalogue TRIM regulations issued by various Governments.

1. The United States Department of Commerce Benchmark surveys

The United States Department of Commerce surveyed investment performance requirements in 1977 and 1982. The results are tabulated in tables 2 and 3. Unlike some of the studies examined later in this chapter, the 1977 and 1982 surveys depended upon transnational corporations reporting how many of their overseas affiliates were subject to various TRIM requirements. The 1977 and 1982 data are not directly comparable since companies with sales of less than $3 million were not included in the 1982 survey (hence tables 2 and 3 have been kept separate). There are three major conclusions:

- As shown in tables 2 and 3, 1 per cent of United States foreign affiliates were subject to minimum export requirements and/or minimum import requirements and/or minimum local content requirements in the developed market economies. In the developing countries, 3 per cent of United States foreign affiliates were subject to minimum export requirements. Three to five per cent were subject to maximum import limits, and 2 to 6 per cent were subject to minimum local content requirements. Adjusting for overlaps, TRIMs of all types affected no more than 3 per cent of the overseas affiliates of larger United States firms (with more than $3 million in sales) and no more than 6 per cent of the overseas affiliates of all United States firms.

Table 2. United States Department of Commerce study: percentage of United States foreign affiliates subject to performance requirements a/
(Percentage)

Item	*Total world*	*Developed market economies*	*Developing countries*
Affiliates subject to:			
Minimum export requirements	2	1	3
Minimum import limits	3	1	5
Minimum local content requirements	3	1	6

Source: United States Department of Commerce, International Trade Administration (ITA) "The use of investment incentives and performance requirements by foreign Governments" (Washington, ITA, 1981).

a/ Percentages cannot be cumulated as one affiliate may be subject to multiple performance requirements.

Table 3. United States Department of Commerce study: incidence of performance requirements and investment incentives among United States foreign affiliates, 1982 a/

(Percentage)

	All industries	
Measure	*Developed market economies*	*Developing countries*
Performance requirements		
Export requirements	1	3
Import limits	0.5	3
Local content usage	0.6	2
Employment requirements	4	15
Transfer-of-technology requirements	2	--
Specific export/import ratio requirements	1	3
Investment incentives		
Tax concessions	25	26
Tariff concessions	7	16
Subsidies	18	9
Other	7	9

Source: United States Department of Commerce, *1982 Benchmark Survey Data* (Washington, Government Printing Office, 1985).

a/ Data are not directly comparable to those in table 2 since firms with under $3 million in sales have been excluded in the 1982 survey.

- In these large surveys of firm responses separated by five years, there was a remarkable consistency of findings, especially in local content and export TRIMs. There were no noticeable trends of increasing or decreasing percentages of firms subject to TRIM regulations.

- The percentage of countries employing TRIM regulations for foreign affiliates was higher among the developing countries than among developed countries in the case of local content regulations, import limits and export requirements. With regard to tax concessions, the percentages in developed and developing countries were approximately equal (25 per cent of subsidiaries in the former versus 26 in the latter). As for subsidies, the developed market economies clearly utilized this measure more often (18 per cent of the affiliates versus 9 per cent). Of 17 countries identified by the United States Trade Representative's Office as having "significant occurrences" of local content and export requirements, 13 were developing countries and four were developed countries. Yet, at the time of the assessment (1981), 28 per cent of total United States foreign direct investment was located in those 13 developing countries whereas 72 per cent of the total was located in the four developed countries.

2. *The United States International Trade Commission study*

In 1982, the United States International Trade Commission (ITC) prepared a quantitative examination of the impact of foreign performance requirements on United States trade, production and employment and foreign investment patterns and income for three industries characterized by significant foreign investment. Like the Department of Commerce Benchmark surveys, the ITC study also relied on the responses of United States transnational corporations. The industries singled out by the ITC were motor vehicles, chemicals (including pharmaceuticals) and high-technology goods. The study covered firms that represented 76 per cent of total United States direct investment abroad in motor vehicles and equipment; 70 per cent of total United States direct investment abroad in chemicals and allied products; and 90 per cent of total United States direct investment abroad in office, computing and accounting machines. For reasons of business confidentiality, the full report was never released but most of the results have been reported in interviews. The main findings are:

- Of the 131 affiliates producing motor vehicles and equipment, 54 affiliates (41 per cent) were found to be subject to TRIMs. More than 80 per cent of the United States motor vehicle and motor vehicle equipment manufacturers operating abroad reported having one or more foreign affiliates operating under TRIM requirements (17 firms out of a total 21). Local content requirements were most common (49 affiliates or 37 per cent of total affiliates), followed by import restrictions (40 affiliates or 31 per cent) and export minimums (15 affiliates or 11 per cent). Seventeen countries utilized TRIMs, of which 10 were in the developing world. Two developed countries (Canada and Australia) were particularly heavy users of TRIMs.
- Of the 367 affiliates producing chemicals and allied products, 45 affiliates (12 per cent) were subject to TRIMs. Forty per cent of the United States producers having direct investment abroad reported having at least one affiliate operating under TRIM requirements. Import restrictions were most frequently reported (34 affiliates or 9 per cent of all affiliates), followed by minimum export requirements (15 affiliates or 4 per cent) and local content rules (10 affiliates or 3

per cent). Although chemicals affiliates were subject to TRIM requirements around the world (17 countries), they were most common in developing countries (12 countries).

- Of the 57 affiliates producing office equipment, computers and accounting machines, 11 affiliates (19 per cent) were subject to TRIMs. Approximately one third of the United States office, computing and accounting machines equipment manufacturers operating internationally reported having one or more foreign affiliates operating under TRIM requirements (six firms out of 16). All of the parent firms had affiliates responding to export minimums (eight affiliates), most to import restrictions (eight affiliates of five firms) and half had affiliates obeying local content rules (six affiliates).

3. *The World Bank study*

The International Finance Corporation of the World Bank sponsored a research team headed by Stephen Guisinger which interviewed more than 30 transnational corporations with regard to 74 investment decisions for projects in some 20 developed and developing countries. The study (1985) covered four industries: food processing, automobiles, computers and petrochemicals.

Of this sample, 38 of the 74 cases (51 per cent) were subject to explicit TRIM requirements. With regard to the sectoral breakdown, 9 of the 12 cases in the automobile sector (75 per cent) experienced TRIM requirements. TRIM requirements in the computer industry, in contrast, were infrequent and unimportant. In the food processing industry, 12 of 25 firms (48 per cent) had TRIM requirements. In the petrochemical industry, TRIM requirements have been located most conspicuously in the developed countries that buy the products (Japan, Western Europe) but appeared to be shifting to the developing country producer States.

Explicit performance requirements were more common in developing than developed countries (although as chapters II and III will discuss, this study discovered that "developed countries achieve much the same result using implicit performance requirements" [6]).

---

6 Stephen E. Guisinger and associates, *Investment Incentives and Performance Requirements* (New York, Praeger, 1985).

4. *The 1985 United States Trade Representative data*

In 1986 Harvey Bale and David Walters used data from the office of the United States Trade Representative (USTR) to provide a further sectoral breakdown of TRIM measures. Their results, combined with those of the ITC and World Bank studies, are given in table 4.

Table 4. Trade-related investment measures, by industry, three studies
(Percentage of United States affiliates subject to TRIM requirements in developed and developing countries)

Industry	*ITC study*	*World Bank study*	*1985 USTR study*
Manufacturing			
Automotive and transportation	41	75	27
Chemicals	12	a/	19
Food products		48	21
Computers, office equipment, accounting	19	-	..
Primary and fabricated metals			18
Non-electrical machinery			14
Electrical machinery			21
Other			17
Mining			27
Petroleum			16
Trade			9
Finance, insurance, real estate			8
Other			10

Sources: Harvey Bale and David Walters, "Investment policy aspects of U.S. and global trade interests", *Looking Ahead*, 9 (January 1986), pp. 1-14.

a/ In petrochemicals, the heavy usage of TRIMs in developed countries is beginning to shift to developing countries.

5. *The Overseas Private Investment Corporation study*

The Overseas Private Investment Corporation (OPIC), an agency of the Government of the United States, examines TRIMs in determining whether a particular investment qualifies for OPIC insurance or funding. The general findings as to extent and characteristics in 682 projects (as of 1987) are reported in table 5. The table shows that 40 per cent of all OPIC projects were

Table 5. OPIC experience with trade-related investment measures, 1987 a/
(Percentage)

Industry	*TRIM requirements*	*No TRIM requirements*
By region:		
All countries	40	60
Middle East	50	50
East Asia	41	59
South Asia	41	59
Caribbean and Latin America	33	67
Africa	28	72
By industry:		
All industries	40	60
Minerals and energy	75	25
Manufacturing	45	55
Construction and services	38	62
Agribusiness and food	24	76
Banking and finance	-	100

Source: Theodore H. Moran and Charles Pearson, *Trade-related Investment Performance Requirements* (Washington, D.C., OPIC, 1987).

a/ 682 projects.

subject to some TRIM requirements, with the highest proportion in the Middle East and the lowest in Africa.

In evaluating these results and comparing them to other studies, it is important to note that the domain of OPIC projects is not congruent with the entire spectrum of United States foreign direct investment. For example, OPIC does not offer insurance for projects in Mexico and Venezuela. In addition, OPIC is required by law to decline assistance to those projects which could potentially have an adverse affect on United States employment, so that entire industries (such as the automobile industry) are absent as OPIC participants. Within the universe of the OPIC sample, minerals and energy were most likely to be subject to TRIM requirements, and banking and finance least likely.

In an effort to refine these data, a sample of 50 OPIC projects was examined on the basis of the following eight questions:

1) Are there any TRIM requirements that may affect this investment?

2) If yes, do they appear to be local content, export or balancing-of-imports-and-exports type requirements?

3) For local content-type requirements, does the regulation suggest that, *ceteris paribus*, a preference be given for domestic inputs (e.g., when price, quality, terms are equal)?

4) Do the TRIM requirements appear to be the result of general regulations or specific to this particular investment?

5) Do the TRIM requirements set numerical targets (percentage or absolute)?

6) Does the firm receive investment incentives or other favourable treatment in return for its trade performance?

7) Are the TRIM requirements binding or redundant?

8) What is the principal reason for OPIC's determination? (All of the projects were approved.)

The results of this examination appear in tables 6 and 7. It should be noted that not every question could be answered with certainty. The projects in this study were concentrated in Central America and the Caribbean (40 per cent) and in Asia (24 per cent), with the others distributed between Africa and the Middle East. The following points are particularly noteworthy:

- TRIM requirements were present in 48 per cent of the projects, with some combination of export and import requirements most frequent (50 per cent of TRIM projects). A balancing of imports and exports was required in 29 per cent of those projects subject to TRIMs. Of the 17 projects in which some import limit or local content requirement occurred, 10 stipulated that domestic products were to be used if available at comparable price and quality (*ceteris paribus* basis).

- Only two of the projects appeared to be subject to TRIMs that were specific to the project and not the result of more general legislation, although the precise requirements might be tailored to the project in many of the other cases.

Table 6. OPIC sample, 1987

Case number	Region	Industry	Question							
			1	*2*	*3*	*4*	*5*	*6*	*7*	*8*
1.	Africa	Lumber & Wood products	Y	B	N	G	Y,M	Y	NB	R
2.	Central America & Caribbean	Horticulture	Y	X	NA	G	N	Y	NB	NXUS
3.	Central America & Caribbean	Horticulture	N							
4.	Middle East	Chemicals	N							
5.	Asia	Electrical equipment	N							
6.	Middle East	Construction	N							
7.	Asia	Glass	Y	M,X,B	N	S	Y,X	N	BIND	NUSXD
8.	Africa	Lumber & Wood products	Y	M,X,B	N	G	N	Y	NB	R
9.	Asia	Chemicals	N							
10.	Central America & Caribbean	Hotels	N							
11.	Asia	Food products	Y	X,M	?	S	Y,X	N	NB	R
12.	Asia	Food products	Y	M,B	Y	G	N	N	NB	NUSXD
13.	Central America & Caribbean	Agricultural crops	Y	M,X	Y	G	N	Yx	NB	R
14.	Central America & Caribbean	Miscellaneous manufactures	N							
15.	Central America & Caribbean	Horticulture	Y	X	NA	G	N	Y	NB	R
16.	Central America & Caribbean	Agricultural crops	Y	X	NA	G	N	Y	NB	R
17.	Africa	Electrical equipment	N							
18.	Latin America	Hotels	Y	M	N	G	N	N	NB	R
19.	Africa	Chemicals	Y	M	?	G	N	N	NB	R
20.	Africa	Metal mining	N							
21.	Central America & Caribbean	Metal mining	N							
22.	Central America & Caribbean	Hotels	N							
23.	Central America & Caribbean	Hotels	N							
24.	Central America & Caribbean	Wholesale trade	N							
25.	Middle East	Chemicals	N							
26.	Asia	Hotels	Y	M	Y	G	N	N	NB	R
27.	Latin America	Oil & gas extraction	Y	M	Y	G	N	N	NB	NUSXD
28.	Central America & Caribbean	Hotels	N							
29.	Latin America	Wholesale trade	Y	X	NA	G	N	Y	BIND	XUSDOUSM

/.....

Table 6. *(continued)*

Case number	*Region*	*Industry*	*Question*							
			1	*2*	*3*	*4*	*5*	*6*	*7*	*8*
30.	Africa	Electrical equipment	N							
31.	Middle East	Fabricated metal products	N							
32.	Asia	Business services	N							
33.	Central America & Caribbean	Apparel and textiles	Y	X	NA	G	N	Y	NB	R
34.	Central America & Caribbean	Hotels	N							
35.	Asia	Chemicals	N							
36.	Asia	Food products	Y	X,M,B	Y	G	N	Y	NB	R
37.	Central America & Caribbean	Fabricated metal products	Y	X,M	Y	G	N	Y	NB	R
38.	Latin America	Banking	N							
39.	Central America & Caribbean	Electrical equipment	Y	X	NA	G	N	Y	NB	R
40.	Central America & Caribbean	Agricultural crops	Y	X,M	Y	G	N	Y	NB	R
41.	Latin America	Business services	N							
42.	Central America & Caribbean	Electrical equipment	N							
43.	Asia	Miscellaneous manufactures	Y	X,M,B	?	G	Y	Y	NB	R
44.	Central America & Caribbean	Fish and shellfish	Y	X,M	Y	G	Y	Y	NB	R
45.	Central America & Caribbean	Agricultural crops	N							
46.	Asia	Chemicals	Y	X,M,B	Y	G	Y	N	BIND	NUSXD
47.	Asia	Business services	N							
48.	Latin America	Paper products	Y	X	NA	G	Y	Y	BIND	NUSXD
49.	Latin America	Finance and insurance	N							
50.	Latin America	Petroleum services	Y	M	Y	G	N	N	NB	R

Source: Theodore H. Moran and Charles Pearson, *Trade-related Investment Performance Requirements* (Washington, D.C., OPIC, 1987).

Key:

Y	Yes.	BIND	Binding TRIM requirement.
N	No.	ok	approved by OPIC.
B	Balancing of exports and imports.	R	Redundant.
X	Export requirements.	NXUS	No significant exports to United States.
M	Restriction on imports (including local content).	NUSXD	No significant United States exports displaced.
G	General TRIM requirement.	XUSDOUSM	Exports to United States displace other United States imports.
S	Specific to the project.	NA	Not applicable.
NB	Not binding TRIM requirement.	?	Unclear.

Table 7. OPIC sample: summary
(Percentage)

Percentage distribution of projects	
Central America and Caribbean	40
Asia	24
Africa	12
Middle East	8
Percentage of projects subject to TRIMs	48
Percentage of TRIM projects subject to	
Local content	21
Export minimum	29
Both, or balancing	50
Percentage of TRIM projects subject to numerical requirements	29
Percentage of TRIM requirements linked to benefits	63
Percentage of TRIM projects in which requirements are redundant	83

Source: Theodore H. Moran and Charles Pearson, *Trade-related Investment Performance Requirements* (Washington, D.C., OPIC, 1987).

- Twenty-nine per cent of the projects subject to TRIMs set numerical targets. In 63 per cent of the TRIM cases, investors received favourable treatment in return for compliance with TRIM regulations.

6. *The 1989 United States Trade Representative survey*

As part of the preparations for the Uruguay Round trade negotiations, the Office of the United States Trade Representative (USTR) prepared in 1989 a survey of TRIMs in 51 countries (31 "middle income and less developed countries" and 20 "developed countries") where TRIMs are particularly likely to be present (49 of the 51 countries) and United States investment is comparatively high. This is a shorter list of countries than that released by the USTR in its inventory in 1985 (92 countries). Ten TRIMs are catalogued, including local content requirements, export requirements, trade-balancing requirements, technology-transfer requirements, exchange restrictions and remittance requirements, licensing requirements, local equity requirements, product-mandating requirements, manufacturing requirements/limitations and investment incentives. The data appear to be drawn from legal and regulatory instruments, without indicating the extent to which they applied in actual projects. The data are summarized in tables 8 and 9. They reflect an arbitrary

Table 8. United States Trade Representative 1989 survey: trade-related investment measures, by type of TRIM, 1989
(Number)

Trade-related investment measure	*Developing countries a/ (of 31 countries)*	*Developed countries b/ (of 20 countries*
Local content	23	6
Export performance	16	3
Trade balancing	1	1
Local equity	17	7
Licensing	10	2
Exchange restrictions or remittance requirements	16	5
Incentives (all)	14	12
Incentives (tied to local content)	7	4
Incentives (tied to export performance)	12	3
Incentives (tied to local equity)	9	1
Other measures		
Technology transfer	11	1
Manufacturing limitation/	5	0
requirement	5	3
Research and Development	0	2
Product mandating		

Source: USTR computerized survey, 1989.
Note: The data exclude the United States.

a/ The 31 "developing countries" are Argentina, Bolivia, Brazil, Cameroon, Central African Republic, Chile, Colombia, Ecuador, Egypt, Ghana, India, Indonesia, Côte d'Ivoire, Jamaica, Kenya, Republic of Korea, Malaysia, Mexico, Morocco, Nigeria, Pakistan, Peoples Republic of China, Peru, Portugal, Singapore, Taiwan Province of China, Thailand, Turkey, Uruguay, Venezuela, Yugoslavia.

b/ The 20 "developed countries" are Australia, Austria, Belgium, Canada, Denmark, Finland, France, Germany, Greece, Ireland, Italy, Japan, Luxembourg, Netherlands, New Zealand, Norway, Spain, Sweden, Switzerland, United Kingdom.

division between "middle income and less developed countries" and "developed countries", with (for example) Portugal and Turkey included in the former.

In the "middle income and less developed countries" category, 23 countries have local content TRIMs and 16 have export TRIMs, with an additional country entered as having "trade balancing" TRIMs. Eleven countries have TRIMs specially designated for the automotive industry and five for electronics and informatics. On the one hand, the range of industries affected by TRIMs is broad (including such industries as fisheries, banking, telecommunications, aircraft, and armaments). On the other hand, the number of countries with TRIMs for designated industries is relatively low. There is, however, a list of 25 countries with TRIMs listed as applying to "all industries".

Table 9. United States Trade Representative 1989 survey: trade-related investment measures, by industry, 1989
(Number)

Trade-related investment measure	*Developing countries a/ (of 31 countries)*	*Developed countries b/ (of 20 countries)*
All industries	25	17
Specific industries c/		
Agriculture	4	1
Automotive	11	2
Banking	3	1
Electronics	3	1
Informatics	2	1
Insurance	1	0
Mining	4	2
Petroleum	6	1
Pharmaceutical	3	1
Other		
Telecommunications	2	1
Aircraft	1	0
Capital goods	2	0
Consumer goods	1	0
Shipping	1	0
Tourism	1	0
Fisheries	4	0
Services	1	0
Construction	1	0
Agricultural equipment	1	0
Textiles	1	0
Armaments	1	0
Iron and steel	1	0
Tobacco	1	0
Civil aviation	0	1
Broadcasting/media	0	1
Financial services	0	1
Services	0	1
Energy	0	1
Publishing	0	1
Selected industry	0	1

Source: USTR computerized survey, 1989.
Note: The data exclude the United States.

a/ The 31 "developing countries" are Argentina, Bolivia, Brazil, Cameroon, Central African Republic, Chile, Colombia, Ecuador, Egypt, Ghana, India, Indonesia, Côte d'Ivoire, Jamaica, Kenya, Republic of Korea, Malaysia, Mexico, Morocco, Nigeria, Pakistan, Peoples Republic of China, Peru, Portugal, Singapore, Taiwan Province of China, Thailand, Turkey, Uruguay, Venezuela, Yugoslavia.

b/ The 20 "developed countries" are Australia, Austria, Belgium, Canada, Denmark, Finland, France, Germany, Greece, Ireland, Italy, Japan, Luxembourg, Netherlands, New Zealand, Norway, Spain, Sweden, Switzerland, United Kingdom.

c/ Does not duplicate "all industries".

In the "developed countries" category, six countries have local content TRIMs and three have export TRIMs, with an additional country entered as "trade balancing". Two countries have TRIMs specially designated for the automotive industry and one for electronics and informatics. Seventeen countries are listed as having TRIMs which apply to "all industries". One should note that the United States does not include its own possible TRIMs in the list (banking, fisheries, shipping). In addition, Japan is simply described as having TRIMs in "sensitive" industries, with no further breakdown.

C. Conclusions

Five conclusions emerge on the extent and characteristics of TRIM requirements. Three are relatively straightforward; two require more careful interpretation.

- *Categories of industry.* There appears to be a wide difference among industries in the incidence of specifically designated TRIM requirements. In all studies the automotive industry appears to be a prime target (27 per cent of United States overseas automotive affiliates surveyed in the Department of Commerce Benchmark survey, 75 per cent of the World Bank automotive sample, more than 80 per cent of the automotive subsidiaries in the ITC sample). For food processing, the World Bank study found 48 per cent of the projects subject to TRIMs. In chemicals and petrochemicals, the World Bank study found a large number (no precise figure given) with TRIM requirements; the ITC survey found 12 per cent. In computers and office equipment, the ITC study discovered 19 per cent of the projects with TRIM requirements; the Guisinger study suggested TRIMs were infrequent and unimportant. Complicating the findings, however, the USTR lists 42 of 51 countries as having TRIM regulations applying to "all industries".

- *Categories of TRIM requirements.* In automobiles and chemicals, local content TRIMs are generally more prevalent than export minimums. In computers and office equipment, export minimums are more prevalent (ITC study). In chemicals and petrochemicals, both local content and export performance TRIMS are used. The sample of OPIC cases suggests that, when TRIMs are used, export and import requirements are frequently combined and export and import balancing is frequent. The OPIC sample also suggests that local content requirements are often required only if inputs of comparable price and quality are available (*ceteris paribus* stipulation). Finally, the

OPIC sample showed that when TRIMs are required, they are often compensated for by other types of favourable treatment (63 per cent).

- *Categories of countries.* TRIMs were found in both developed and developing countries. TRIMS are more likely to be found in developing countries than in developed countries, and there is a greater number of the former with TRIMs than the latter. Nevertheless, there may be "implicit" TRIMs which are not widely recorded in conventional studies. Debates about "rules of origin" in the European Community (and elsewhere) are essentially negotiations about local value-added requirements. The controversy about whether the Government of France would count Bluebird cars imported from the Nissan plant in the United Kingdom as part of the parent company's non-European import quota into France, or alternatively as a European-built car, for example, revolved around whether the 70 per cent United Kingdom local content of the Bluebird would satisfy the French minimum of 80 per cent.[7]

The final two conclusions require more detailed analysis.

- *Coverage of investors.* In contrast to the raw data on numbers of countries with TRIMs on the books, the data on coverage of investors suggests that developed country regulations cover more breadth of investment. Using the USTR information on United States direct investment in each country (in 1987, the latest available year) as a proxy to measure the extent of investment potentially touched by TRIMs, the amount of United States investment covered by local content and trade-balancing TRIMs is $24 billion in the "middle income developing countries", and $125 billion in the "developed countries". The corresponding figures for United States investments potentially affected by export TRIMs are $17 billion in the former and $72 billion in the latter. United States investments potentially affected by incentives amount to $195 billion in "developed countries" and $11 billion in "middle income developing countries". For those countries where there is a listing of TRIMs applied to "all industries", the comparative figures are $38 billion in the "middle income developing countries" and $212 billion in the "developed countries". Finally, the amount of United States investment in the countries with the most extensive presence of TRIM regulations is

7 UNCTC, "Trade-related aspects of intellectual property rights and trade-related investment measures" (E/C.10/1990/13, 7 March 1990), p. 16.

$30 billion in the top 20 "middle income developing countries", versus $230 billion in the top 20 "developed countries".

Table 10 summarizes the data showing that TRIMs cover four to 17 times more investment in the developed countries than in the developing countries. This result was confirmed as well in the 1982 Commerce Department study, where developing country TRIMs were more prevalent but five developed countries using TRIMs had much larger affiliate operations (72 per cent of the total capital in a sample of 17 countries).

- *Incidence*. It is a challenge to determine the actual incidence of TRIMs. There is a wide disparity among studies which report, or infer, the frequency of TRIM usage. In the case of the developing countries, for example, the more comprehensive surveys (1977 and 1982 United States Department of Commerce benchmarks) found a total of no more than 6 per cent of United States foreign affiliates subject to TRIM requirements (taking overlaps into account). The much narrower OPIC survey, however, discovered 40 per cent of the small sample subject to TRIMs. The World Bank study recorded 51 per cent on an even smaller number of cases subject to TRIM requirements. The USTR survey of government regulations found 49

Table 10. Developed and developing countries: number of countries with trade-related investment measures vs. amount of United States investment covered by TRIMs
(In billions of dollars)

	Developed countries		*Developing countries*	
Trade-related investment measure	*Number of countries*	*Amount of United States investment covered*	*Number of countries*	*Amount of United States investment covered*
Local content a/	7	125	24	24
Export requirements a/	4	72	17	17
Incentives	12	195	14	11
All industries	17	212	25	38
Top 20 TRIM users	20	230	20	30

Source: Compiled from USTR computerized survey data, 1989.

of 51 countries with TRIMs of which 42 were reported having TRIMs covering "all industries".

Table 11 records the disparity between the 45 per cent to 62 per cent of the investment in the developing countries being reported to "be covered by" local content or export TRIMs, and the 2 per cent to 6 per cent of affiliates reporting being actually "subject to" local content or export TRIMs.

Two complementary explanations suggest themselves.

- First, the majority of the TRIMs hypothetically in force in various countries may be discretionary and negotiable, with firms not having to comply if the terms are too onerous (or if they are in a strong enough bargaining position to resist). This would reconcile the otherwise conflicting evidence that a large number of countries with a great deal of foreign direct investment within their borders have TRIMs on the books, while most of the investors do not report that their subsidiaries are governed by TRIMs. This explanation is consistent with data released by the USTR in 1985, where 58 per cent of the TRIMs in 91 countries were reported to be discretionary and negotiable. [8]

Table 11. Developing countries: investors "subject to" trade-related investment measures vs. investment "covered by" TRIMs

Trade-related investment measure	*Percentage of affiliates (1977)*	*Percentage of affiliates (1982)*	*Percentage of countries (of 31 in 1988)*	*Percentage of investment (of 31 in 1988)*
Local content	6	2	58	62
Export requirement	3	3	55	45

Source: Compiled from USTR computerized survey data, 1989.

Note: The years are not the same, but there is no reason to suspect a dramatic shift in government practice between 1982 and 1988.

8 United States Trade Representative, Office of Investment Policy, "Inventory of investment barriers", 22 October 1985.

- Second, the majority of the TRIMs may not require the investor to undertake actions the parent firm finds uneconomic and/or is not planning to undertake anyway (such TRIMs are redundant). This would explain why even the large number of firms operating in countries where TRIMs were actually in force did not consider themselves "subject to TRIM requirements". This interpretation of the evidence finds support in the OPIC study, in which 83 per cent of the projects subject to TRIMs merely required the investors to carry out activities (local sourcing, exporting) which they planned to do on their own (see table 7). Similarly, in the World Bank study, corporate officers reported in several of the 38 cases subject to TRIMs that their subsidiaries would eventually have achieved the specified levels of exports or domestic content; the TRIMs merely accelerate the firms' plans to develop local suppliers and enter export markets.[9]

These five conclusions about the incidence and characteristics of TRIM requirements are important in evaluating the impact of TRIMs on patterns of trade and development (chapter II) and assessing the implications for policy (chapter III).

9 Guisinger and associates, op. cit.

II. The impact of trade-related investment measures on trade and development: theory and evidence

The literature on TRIMs includes few efforts to analyse empirically the impact of such measures on trade and development. In part, this is due to the difficulty, as the second section of this chapter points out, of conducting the proper tests to measure distortion. But it is also due to an unquestioned theoretical framework which has assured analysts in the past that TRIMS by their very nature could lead to no other outcome except distortion.

In recent years, there have been advances in both theory and evidence. The challenge, as this chapter and the next will show, is to bring contemporary policy analysis up to the level of sophistication of the current generation of analytical work in the field.

This chapter reviews the principal theoretical frameworks within which the impact of TRIMs on trade and development can be judged. It then examines the evidence, both with regard to which framework is more suitable and what the impact of TRIMs actually appears to be. It concludes with a summary of findings to lay the basis for examining policy implications in chapter III.

A. Theory

There are two principal frameworks for analysing the impact of TRIMs: the neo-classical framework of perfect competition, and the newer "strategic trade" framework of oligopoly and imperfect competition. The TRIMs debate demonstrates how important the choice of an appropriate theoretical framework is for designing policy responses.

1. Trade-related investment measures in neo-classical theory

The conventional way to look at TRIMs is within neo-classical assumptions of perfect competition. Most policy analysis of the impact of TRIMs on trade and development is wedded to this framework. [10]

In the neo-classical analysis, firms are too small and too numerous to influence market conditions. Instead, they merely react to market signals, allocating resources to the most productive uses in their drive to maximize profits. Other than profit-maximization, corporations cannot be said to have a strategy *per se*: they have no leeway or discretion about the conduct of their own operations; they are unable to collect economic rents. An emerging opportunity or technological breakthrough may raise profits above some "normal" level for a moment, but successive waves of entrepreneurs rush in, driving excess profits back down to the normal level. Within the neo-classical framework, government intervention in the marketplace to influence where and how production takes place, except to correct for negative social externalities (e.g., pollution), produces distortion in economic activity.

The conventional case against TRIMs comes from extending the neo-classical presumption against public intervention to international markets, asserting that protection and promotion create distortions in the pattern of both trade and development. Only in unusual circumstances can a departure from free trade be justified with any rigour, e.g., a possible "optimal tariff" on the part of a country that uses a large enough share of the output of a commodity to turn the terms of trade in that country's favour. (For infant industry considerations, see below.) [11]

Before turning to revisionist perspectives on trade interventionism, it is worthwhile to look closely at the criticism of the most visible forms of TRIM intervention, domestic content and export requirements (perhaps combined in trade-balancing regulations), within the conventional framework. A TRIM requirement which mandates a certain amount of domestic content on the part of foreign investors, like any other form of import protection, raises the cost

---

10 A lucid (non-mathematical) treatment of trade theory and options for public intervention is W.M. Corden, *Trade Policy and Economic Welfare* (Oxford, Oxford University Press, 1974).

11 Trade restrictions can also be used to correct domestic distortions or alter income distribution. The common conclusion is that such policy objectives are better handled via other policy instruments. See J. Bhagwati, "The generalized theory of distortions and welfare", in J. Bhagwati *et al.*, eds., *Trade, Balance of Payments and Growth* (Amsterdam, North-Holland, 1971); and A. Dixit, "Tax policy in open economies", in A. Auerbach and M. Feldstein, eds., *The Handbook of Public Economics* (Amsterdam, North-Holland, 1984).

of production to the subsidiaries upon which it is imposed, reducing consumption and withdrawing resources that could be more productively used elsewhere in the economy. Adding to the inefficiencies inflicted by the TRIM requirement upon domestic production and consumption, Richard Brecher and Carlos Diaz Alejandro have pointed out that foreign capital in the protected sector is likely to increase its rate of return, resulting in a process of "immiserizing growth" as foreign firms capture excess profits at the expense of local consumers unless the profits are entirely taxed away (an unlikely outcome).[12]

A TRIM requirement to export exacerbates the problem. Within the neo-classical model, output costs in the local market must by definition be higher than world prices or else domestic subsidiaries of foreign corporations would be exporting on their own. Consequently, with the export requirement must come a public subsidy to induce the firm to respond, imposing a tax of sorts on the public, and reducing consumption further. The subsidy then draws more resources into the inefficient sector, intensifying the misallocation of resources in the first place. As for export-led growth via "balancing" domestic content and export requirements, Gene Grossman has found that a domestic content scheme adopted to improve the trade account may actually worsen it by reducing the export potential of the domestic industry.[13]

For these reasons, it is not difficult to understand why the neo-classical economic tradition is critical of domestic content and export-promotion TRIMs: both appear undesirable from the host country as well as from the home country and global perspectives. TRIMs misallocate resources in the local market, thwarting development, and preventing countries (including the host country which employs the TRIMs) from being able to benefit from international comparative advantage.

In conventional trade theory, there is one exception to the presumption against intervening in the international market-allocation process: the familiar infant-industry case. The infant-industry argument is built upon relaxing

---

12 Interestingly, the immiserizing outcome does not depend upon the assumption that foreign firms transfer their higher profits home. See Richard A. Brecher and Carlos F. Diaz Alejandro, "Tariffs, foreign capital and immiserizing growth", *Journal of International Economics*, 7 (1977), pp. 317-322.

13 Gene Grossman, "The theory of domestic content protection and content preference", *Quarterly Journal of Economics* (November 1981), pp. 583-604. On the other hand, developing countries frequently face a tariff structure which discriminates against processed raw materials. In such a situation, export incentives could be needed to offset such discrimination, as in the case of Korean protection of plywood manufacture. The outcome could be a more efficient allocation of resources internationally with the export TRIM than without.

neo-classical assumptions about perfect markets in one area: the acquisition of experience. Here, one hypothesizes that there may be a learning curve advantage from becoming familiar with production and sales from a local base, an advantage that any single investor cannot later fully recoup as others enter the industry without incurring the first entrant's start-up costs. To overcome this market imperfection which prevents the launching of a domestic industry, temporary public support may be justified. (Economists would recommend a subsidy rather than a tariff.) Conventional trade theory is sceptical of the infant-industry argument, however, for three reasons: first, there is scepticism about the extensiveness of market failure which would justify the public intervention in the first place; second, there is scepticism about the ability of governmental authorities to choose appropriately which industries should be protected or promoted; and third, there is scepticism about providing resources at public expense to interest groups which may want to remain in diapers indefinitely rather than grow up to survive on their own. Moreover, within the analysis of domestic content and export promotion above (see the reference to the work of Grossman), the expansion of production of the final goods needed to provide valuable "learning by doing" may not take place; instead, contraction may result.

Finally, following from assertions that TRIMs misallocate resources both domestically and internationally, there is a larger systemic argument about the necessity to prohibit domestic content and export-promotion schemes. Since under neo-classical conditions firm behaviour is determined exogenously, governmental interference as to where to produce, what inputs to use and where to market are certain to produce large swings in firm activity. An international trade regime that does not prevent domestic content regulations and export requirements from multiplying would allow transnational corporations to be jerked about by such regulations, chasing after markets their competitors would fill if they did not. The result would be much wasteful shifting of productive activities, leading to a lower level of economic welfare for developed and developing countries alike.

Thus, the neo-classical framework comes down quite harshly on the idea of TRIMs as having any benefit for the countries that employ them, and urges that TRIMs (especially domestic content or export TRIMs) be proscribed as tools for development policy or trade enhancement.

To evaluate the extent to which the neo-classical paradigm is relevant for policy analysis, one will want to scrutinize the evidence later in this chapter to determine whether perfect or imperfect competition is the more accurate characterization of the industries in which trade and foreign direct investment take place. Similarly, to evaluate the extent to which the trade system itself is being undermined by TRIMs, one will want to examine empirically the severity with which domestic content and export requirements actually produce shifts in the location of production.

2. Trade-related investment measures and strategic trade theory

Strategic trade theory moves beyond the neo-classical paradigm. Avinash Dixit described the need for the economics discipline to refocus its perspective in his Frank Paish lecture before the Royal Economic Society at Oxford:

> Almost all the received theory of international trade, positive and normative, is based on the model of atomistic competition .... In reality, it is becoming increasingly evident that a significant proportion of international trade takes place in imperfectly competitive markets. Here the individual producers and sellers are aware of their monopoly power, and act to profit from it. The resulting market equilibrium, be it pure monopoly, oligopoly, or monopolistic competition, differs from the textbook Walrasian kind. The determinants and patterns of trade are different, and are differently affected by commercial policy. A new framework of theoretical analysis is therefore required for proper understanding of many current issues of trade, and of trade policy.[14]

Strategic trade analysis centres on industries in which there are market imperfections and barriers to the entry of competitors. It concentrates on public policy in second-best contexts where only a relatively small number of firms exist, with oligopolistic interactions among them.

In the developed countries, strategic trade theory has been used to nurture domestic firms in such industries as semiconductors, supercomputers and aerospace. In a dramatic turnabout from free trade thinking, the arguments of the strategic trade school are being invoked, in the advanced industrial States, to justify public intervention to shift production locations and trade patterns in favour of home country advantage.

At the same time, however, there is considerable concern in the economics community that strategic trade theory may be used to justify an epidemic of

14 Avinash Dixit, "International trade policy for oligopolistic industries", supplement to the *Economic Journal*, vol. 94 (1984), p 1. The seminal work in developing strategic trade theory is by two Canadians, James A. Brander and Barbara J. Spencer, "International R&D rivalry and industrial strategy", *Review of Economic Studies*, 50 (1983), pp 707-722.

special pleading for protection and promotion which runs contrary to market-based competition. Jagdish Bhagwati has argued that the dangers of imperfect competition are best served by increasing trade liberalization, not reducing it.[15] David Richardson showed that the impact of external competition is even more advantageous in settings of potential oligopoly than in settings of perfect competition.[16] And Paul Krugman, one of the pioneers of strategic trade theory, warned: "there is a risk that interest groups that have a stake in trade policy will simply find in new ideas an excuse to advocate policies that are not likely to benefit the nation as a whole".[17]

What can be extracted from strategic trade theory to enlighten the understanding of TRIMs, especially domestic content and export-promotion TRIMs, as they affect patterns of trade and development for developing countries?

There are two (related) strands of argument of particular relevance to developing countries: strategic trade theory posits, first, that properly constructed public intervention on the part of host country authorities can shift rents from parent corporations to host country tax authorities and/or host country consumers; second (an extension of the rent-shifting idea above), that properly constructed public intervention on the part of host country authorities can transfer production from home country or third country locales to roughly equivalent (or superior) locales in the host country, improving host country welfare (and also, perhaps, home country and global welfare at the same time). On the other hand, as indicated above, improperly constructed public policies can have a disproportionately malign impact on trade and development.[18] Strategic trade theory thus leaves public policy analysts with a more daunting task than neo-classical trade theory: under conditions of imperfect competition, the outcome from public intervention cannot be assumed to be automatically undesirable or distortionary, but neither can it be assumed to be beneficial or welfare-enhancing. There is no substitute for a detailed analysis of the conditions for and nature of each kind of intervention.

It is useful to follow each line of argument on behalf of strategic trade intervention in more detail. For rent-shifting to be feasible, one only need assume the presence of imperfect competition in the industries in which international trade and investment take place, generating oligopoly rents for

---

15 Bhagwati, *Protectionism*, op. cit.

16 Richardson, op. cit.

17 Paul Krugman, ed., *Strategic Trade Policy and the New International Economics* (Cambridge, Mass., The MIT Press, 1986), p. 19.

18 See, Richardson, op. cit.

the firms in those industries. A developing country with no domestic competitors can capture some of these oligopoly rents by imposing a tariff: under plausible conditions (constant marginal costs for the foreign firms and a domestic demand curve which is not too convex), the tariff will not be fully passed on in domestic prices, transferring part of the foreign rent to host authorities.[19] Indeed, the optimal interventionist policy would be a fixed fee for right of access with a per-unit import subsidy, inducing the foreign firms to charge their marginal cost and providing greater supply and lower prices for host country consumers than the laissez-faire alternative.

To set the stage for an analysis of TRIMs policy, one must move one step further: what if the foreign firms establish subsidiaries inside the country's protected market without domestic competitors or with competitors which produce at much higher cost? As before, an optimal rent shifting strategy would be to charge a fixed fee for right of establishment with a production subsidy to push the foreign subsidiaries out to their marginal cost curve. But the final-good-producing foreign subsidiaries may exercise monopsonistic power *vis-à-vis* local suppliers, driving down prices and reducing output. This will result in an underutilization of domestic components. The first-best solution to remedy the problem of underutilization might be a subsidy for local component production. If such a subsidy were impracticable, for economic or political reasons, a domestic content TRIM requirement would emerge as a second-best alternative.[20]

In sum, an activist trade policy involving protection-cum-domestic content TRIMs becomes an acceptable means of reducing the impact of oligopoly

---

19 The argument is reminiscent of the familiar optimal tariff reasoning, in which the tariff results (in part) in improved terms of trade rather than higher domestic prices. To achieve this result in the case of foreign oligopolistic firms, however, the local market does not have to be large in relation to global markets (as must be the case for a country to affect its terms of trade via a tariff). The analysis here follows Paul Krugman, "New trade theory and the less developed countries", in Guillermo Calvo, ed., *Debt, Stabilization, and Development* (Cambridge, Mass., B. Blackwell for WIDER, 1989).

20 This is the model developed by Martin Richardson, "The effects of a content requirement on a foreign duopolist", *The Journal of International Economics*, forthcoming, 1991. See also Neil Vousden, "Content protection and tariffs under monopoly and competition", *Journal of International Economics* (Netherlands), 23 (November 1987), pp. 263-282; and Kala Krishna and Motoshige Itoh, "Content protection and oligopolistic interactions", National Bureau of Economic Research, Working Paper No. 1843, February 1986.

power enjoyed by international investors and correcting for their distortions in local markets.[21]

To move a step further to the idea of production-shifting (or production-establishing), one must add to the assumption of imperfect competition the presence of increasing returns to scale and dynamic gains from learning-by-doing. Under these conditions, trade protection takes on a much more important role than mere rent-shifting. A reconstituted formulation of the infant-industry argument emerges from that which has acquired the name "import protection as export promotion".[22] Protection against imports in one market provides firms located there a preferential opportunity to reap the benefits of economies of scale, to create or refine technologies associated with large production runs and to work their way along the experience curve of managing large operations, while denying this opportunity to external firms. The lower resulting marginal cost for the protected firms will then give them the edge in international markets. In short, by allowing domestically based firms to move down their marginal cost curves (and, dynamically, down their learning curves), the protected domestic market ultimately serves as a springboard for exports. International investors find themselves in a situation where only a relatively small number of production sites (automotive engine plants, petrochemical facilities or computer fabrication operations, of special interest to developing country authorities; aerospace plants, supercomputer facilities and semiconductor operations, of special interest to developed countries) can supply large portions of world markets; but exactly which production sites those investors choose to occupy is not exogenously determined.

The strategic trade framework thus begins to call into question traditional concepts about comparative advantage. There is a pattern of international production and international trade which is returns-to-scale-driven and only loosely related to inherent resource endowments, population aptitudes and cultural tastes. Moving upstream from final goods, if there are scale economies in the production of intermediate goods, there may be linkage effects between these intermediate goods and their buyers. These lead, as Elhanan Helpman

---

21 Chapter III discusses the difficulty of actually using domestic content TRIMs in the real world in a manner that enhances rather than detracts from host country welfare. Carl Davidson, Steven J. Matusz and Mordechai E. Kreinin found, for example, that if foreign subsidiaries exercise their market power *vis-à-vis* local consumers rather than local suppliers, net host country welfare can fall as the decline in consumer surplus outweighs the shift of producer surplus in the local economy. "Analysis of performance standards for direct foreign investment", *Canadian Journal of Economics*, vol. 18 (November 1985), pp. 876-890.

22 Krugman, ed., op. cit.

and Paul Krugman show, to the formation of "industrial complexes" tying traded and non-traded goods into an inter-industry magnet of global proportions in a single geographical location.[23] Comparative advantage is no longer simply a given state of affairs which public authorities must accept. One begins to encounter in the strategic trade literature the notion that states can "create their own comparative advantage".[24]

In point of fact, creating one's own comparative advantage is an extreme portrayal of reality and, as observed below, a pre-emptive struggle among developed nations of favouring a country's "own" firms in an attempt to disable outsiders has severe drawbacks. But this insight from strategic trade theory alerts public policy analysts to the idea that, for many global industries with increasing returns to scale, there may be a large amount of arbitrary or purely historical determination in the location of production and subsequent flows of trade, and that positive government intervention is required to alter that arbitrariness. Comparative advantage is not irrelevant but, as Krugman characterized it,[25] there is an overlay of semi-random scale-economy specialization on a comparative advantage base, with a great deal of uncertainty about exactly what the comparative advantage base is. There may well be multiple potential production sites of approximately equal cost (and/or where the cost of discovering which of the multiple production sites is optimal is high in comparison to the cost differential); but only in a world of perfect knowledge (and, in some sense, equal learning experience) would the complete range of possibilities be revealed. Imperfections in information markets, as well as potential risk aversion on the part of transnational investors, take on increasing importance.

Thus, under thoroughly plausible conditions of imperfect competition among transnational firms in industries with large economies of scale and potential learning-curve gains (for evidence, see the next section of this chapter), countries which take the international structure of comparative advantage as given may find themselves at a disadvantage in relation to those which attempt to play a more active role in shaping the composition of their economic base. To overcome this disadvantage, TRIMs may have to be

---

23 Elhanan Helpman and Paul Krugman, *Market Structure and Foreign Trade: Increasing Returns, Imperfect Competition, and the International Economy* (Cambridge, Mass., The MIT Press, 1986), chapter 11.

24 See Stephen S. Cohen and John Zysman, *Manufacturing Matters: The Myth of the Post Industrial Economy* (New York, Basic Books, 1987).

25 The analysis here follows Krugman, "New trade theory and the less developed countries", loc. cit.

considered in the effort to influence the location of production, the selection of inputs, the size of operations and the marketing of output.

In comparison to an advanced industrial State, however, the Government of a developing country is unlikely to be on equal footing in playing the game of strategic trade. To work easily, the "import-restriction-as-export-promotion" idea requires a domestic market large enough to allow exploitation of the economies of scale inherent in the industry. In the case of most developing countries, a protected domestic market is likely to be small relative to the minimum efficient size of production, let alone in comparison with any massive economies of scale realizable only if the firm reconfigures itself to serve global markets. Inter-firm dynamics exacerbate the problem by ensuring that the small domestic market is served by several manufacturers, rendering the production run of each firm even smaller. [26] Moreover the experience curve of the small producers is hardly likely to prepare them for global competition; instead their dynamic learning will be centred on trying to offset high inefficiency through compensation from artificial profits in the protected markets (see below for reports of conflicts between parent and subsidiary managers when the former try to restrain exports from the latter).

Moreover, developing countries seldom start with their own national champion aerospace firms, semiconductor producers or automobile companies as the strategic trade literature postulates (and nor do *all* developed countries, for that matter). Instead, they must use as a vehicle foreign subsidiaries whose parents have large investments in facilities and skilled labour in the home country (and other developed country locales). As a result, developing country Governments may have to overcome exit costs from familiar sites and start-up costs at new sites (plus, perhaps, the expense and uncertainty of redesigning plants to utilize different factor proportions), all with foreign controlled oligopolists whose instincts are risk-averse. [27] Section B of this chapter records the difficulties which intra-firm rigidities cause in responding to production opportunities, as when a German firm expressed the fear that increased exports from its developing country subsidiaries could endanger exports from Germany, or when Japanese firms require a

26 Eastman and Stykolt demonstrate that protection will lead to excessive entry into a given industry and result in inefficient plant size; a result frequently observed in developing countries. See H. Eastman and S. Stykolt, "A model for the study of protected oligopolies", *Economic Journal*, 70 (1960), pp. 336-347.

27 Plant redesign could involve more labour intensive facilities or, as a variation, experimentation with semi-automated operations.

gentleman's agreement from local joint venture partners not to interfere with the market preserve of the parent's subsidiaries in other markets.[28]

In a developed country context, strategic trade theorists envision import protection as being a sufficient tool to motivate production-shifting behaviour. If the beggar-thy-neighbour dynamic of using import restrictions to favour national champions comes to appear self-defeating, however — as one observes in the aircraft, supercomputer and semiconductor industries — developed country policy makers are increasingly left with production subsidies as the principal reward to offer to investors for establishing facilities large enough to capture the given economies of scale and (implicitly) alter the trade balance. For developed countries, few economists would jump to the conclusion that some kind of export or trade-balancing TRIM, using access to a protected market as an incentive to motivate export expansion, is the optimal approach.

In the developing country context, however, there may be no other plausible choice. If developing countries lack the option of providing large up-front production subsidies to foreign corporations in the range of $100-$300 million to equal the incentives from developed countries (see chapter III), they may be left with trying to fashion some form of export-oriented TRIM-based strategy.[29]

As in the case of domestic content TRIMs, the choice of a TRIM-based export strategy has drawbacks of its own. The advantages and disadvantages of using TRIMs to maintain oneself as a player in the strategic trade game are assessed in the final chapter.

Appendix B examines with some rigour a model of the public policy interests of a host Government confronted with an imperfectly competitive global industry where there are increasing returns to scale and multiple equivalent production sites. The model follows a formulation developed by Krugman, with help in this adaptation from Martin Richardson. The model illustrates a situation in which a transnational firm can gain a potential rent by setting up operations at any one of a number of comparable cost sites.

---

28 For the German case, see Isaiah Frank, *Foreign Enterprise in Developing Countries* (Baltimore, Johns Hopkins University Press, 1980), p. 104. For the Japanese case, see UNCTC, "Transnational corporations and incentives and performance requirements in foreign direct investment in developing countries: case study of India" (New York, United Nations Centre on Transnational Corporations, 1988), mimeo.

29 Moreover, as Dani Rodrik pointed out, if there are indigenous final goods producers as well as foreign subsidiaries, an export TRIM can shift producer surplus to the indigenous firms. Dani Rodrik, "The economics of export performance requirements", *The Quarterly Journal of Economics*, vol. 102 (August 1987), pp. 633-650.

Simultaneously, the model represents the producer surplus that the country obtains if its own site is chosen for the project; the producer surplus accrues to the host nation in the form of higher earnings for workers and suppliers associated with the project. It demonstrates that a host Government can capture not only the producer surplus but also a large portion of the transnational firm's rent through activist policies, e.g., charging a lump-sum tax for right of establishment. The international company, in fact, should be willing to transfer all of the rent to the host country if it has no other sites for production.

At the same time, however, the potential host authorities should be willing to grant benefits to a transnational investor up to the total amount of the producer surplus to attract the firm to locate its operations within the host country's jurisdiction as opposed to elsewhere. This suggests that there could easily be a subsidy war to attract investment that dissipates not only the rent from the transnational firm but the producer surplus as well. In general, therefore, strategic trade theory encourages an activist use of public policy on the part of individual Governments. The alternative of sitting back and letting an abstract idea such as "market forces" dictate national welfare is hardly prudent. But it warns Governments that the prisoner's dilemma lies ahead: if all follow their own self-interests instead of cooperating to stabilize individual behaviour, they all will end up worse off.

This is a challenge the final chapter will address. But first, looking at the data in the next section: is the neo-classical paradigm or the strategic trade framework a better description of the real world, and to what extent is the competition among potential host countries already becoming apparent?

B. Evidence

What does the evidence indicate about the impact of TRIMs on trade and development?

As the previous section demonstrated, an assessment of how TRIMs affect patterns of trade and development requires several layers of analysis: first, on industry structure; second, on firm response; and third, on economic impact. If one discovers that the competitive structure of industries affected by TRIMs approximates the neo-classical paradigm of perfect competition, one can expect the firm response to be massive (justifying the fear that TRIMs in fact "jerk around" investment flows), and the economic impact to be distortionary to both trade and development. If, in contrast, one discovers that the structure of such industries is imperfectly competitive, one can expect firm response to be more discretionary (corporations have a choice or leeway in determining production location according to their own internal strategies, including, but not limited to, the pursuit of Government-sponsored benefits), and the economic impact to be problematic (depending critically on the design of public policies where the firms operate).

1. Evidence on industry structure

As the previous section indicated, there has been a growing presumption in the economics community that elements of oligopoly may be present in many areas of international transaction. This is particularly true where foreign direct investment is present. Indeed, all the major contemporary explanations of foreign direct investment embody in one form or another the notion that the decision to establish direct control over operations abroad, instead of merely exporting goods or licensing technology, arises from market imperfections. The initial insights of Stephen Hymer, expanded and elaborated by Charles Kindleberger and Raymond Vernon, centred on corporate strategies to extend the extraction of rents from barriers to entry before local entrepreneurs eroded them.[30] Richard Caves incorporated this approach in the idea of "sector-specific capital" which extracts oligopoly profits across borders.[31] Recent researchers (like Oliver Williamson) highlight the difficulties for arm's-length parties of making credible commitments over the distribution of rents, leading to the internalization of rent-generating activities across borders.[32] All told, the essence of transnational corporate operations is derived from the failure of markets to conform with neo-classical standards of competition.

Moving to the evidence, one finds the existence of oligopoly in all the industries where foreign direct investment is present. There is a strong correlation between high concentration ratios and outward investment for the United

30 Stephen H. Hymer, *The International Operations of National Firms: A Study of Direct Foreign Investment* (Cambridge, Mass., The MIT Press, 1976); Charles P. Kindleberger, *American Business Abroad: Six Lectures on Direct Investment* (New Haven, Conn., Yale University Press, 1969); Raymond Vernon, "International investment and international trade in the product cycle", *Quarterly Journal of Economics*, 80 (May 1966), pp. 190-207.

31 Richard E. Caves, *Multinational Enterprise and Economic Analysis* (Cambridge, Mass., Cambridge University Press, 1982).

32 Oliver E. Williamson, *The Economic Institutions of Capitalism* (New York, The Free Press, 1985), chapter 11.

States, the United Kingdom, France and Germany. [33] Turned around, measures of market concentration among host developing countries are even higher. The four-firm concentration ratio is higher than 50 per cent in 83 and 84 per cent of the industries where foreign direct investment has occurred in Brazil and Mexico, for example; concentration ratios have been found to be similarly high in studies of foreign investment in Chile, Colombia and Malaysia. [34]

What about the market structure of the industries surrounding and supporting foreign subsidiaries? Here, data limitations prevent a breakdown in terms of prime and supplier industries, external and indigenous ownership. But it is clear that perfect competition is not the typical case. A compilation of data from six developing countries, across a wide time span, reveals an unmistakable pattern, extending from an average four-firm concentration ratio of 50 per cent in Chile (encompassing 41 industries) to an average four-firm concentration ratio of 73 per cent in Mexico (encompassing 73). For comparative purposes, Rodrik included similar concentration ratios for the United States and France. [35] Table 12 demonstrates that all six developing countries find their local industrial structure more concentrated, for example, than the United States — even though the United States figure comes from a much greater level of disaggregation of industries, biasing it upward in comparison to the other countries. A more comparable test would be to examine two cases where the level of disaggregation is similar, Pakistan and France: the average concentration ratio for Pakistan (66 per cent) is more than twice as large as that for France (28 per cent).

In sum, the data reveal a pervasive presence of market imperfections among the industries in which foreign direct investment originates and where it comes to reside. One loses the justification, therefore, for assuming that firm

---

33 F. Fishwick, *Multinational Companies and Economic Concentration in Europe* (Paris, Institute for Research and Information on Multinationals, 1981); T.A. Pugel, *International Market Linkages and U.S. Marketing: Prices, Profits and Patterns* (Cambridge, Mass., Ballinger, 1978); Peter Buckley and John H. Dunning, "The industrial structure of U.S. indirect investment in the U.K.", *Journal of International Business Studies*, Spring/Summer, XI (1980), pp. 9-22.

34 J. M. Connor, *The Market Power of Multinationals: A Quantitative Analysis of U.S. Corporations in Brazil and Mexico* (New York, Praeger, 1977). For a survey of the data on foreign direct investment and market structure, see Richard Newfarmer, ed., *Profits, Progress and Poverty* (Notre Dame, Indiana, University of Notre Dame Press, 1988), chapter 2.

35 Dani Rodrik, "Imperfect competition, scale economies, and trade policy in developing countries", in Robert E. Baldwin, ed., *Trade Policy Issues and Empirical Analysis* (Chicago, The University of Chicago Press, 1988).

Table 12. Comparison of four-firm concentration ratios in the industries of various countries

Country	*Year*	*Unweighted average of four-firm concentration ratios (Percentage)*	*Number of industries*
Brazil	1972	72	68
Chile	1979	50	41
India	1968	55	22
Mexico	1972	73	73
Pakistan	1968	66	51
Turkey	1976	67	125
United States	1972	40	323
France	1969	28	48

Source: The sources of the data here, compiled by Dani Rodrik, are for Brazil, India, Mexico and Pakistan: from original sources cited by N.H. Leff, "Monopoly capitalism and public policy in developing countries", *Kylos*, 32 (1979) pp. 718-38, table 1; for Chile: Jaime de Melo and Shujiro Urata, "The influence of increased foreign competition on industrial concentration and profitability", *International Journal of Industrial Organization*, 4 (1986), pp. 287-304; for Turkey: Ilhan Tekeli, Selim Ilkin, Ataman Aksoy and Yakup Kepenek, *Turkiye' de sanayi kesiminde yogunlasma* (Concentration in the manufacturing industry in Turkey), Middle East Technical University, Ankara, Turkey; for the United States: F.M. Scherer, *Industrial Market Structure and Economic Performance*, 2nd edition (Boston, Houghton-Mifflin, 1980); for France: Alexis Jacquemin and Henry W. de Jong, *European Industrial Organization* (New York, John Wiley, 1977).

behaviour will allocate resources efficiently on their own across borders (as the neo-classical model predicts), or for presuming that policy intervention on the part of host authorities will automatically lead to distortion.

Under conditions of imperfect competition, transnational corporations will enjoy a certain amount of choice, freedom and leeway about where to locate the various stages of their operations and how to conduct intra-corporate activities. This opens up the prospect of "stickiness" in altering established relations among commonly owned entities. Isaiah Frank reported a case in which a European company feared that exports from a developing country subsidiary would disrupt markets for other units. [36] UNCTC documented the practice on the part of Japanese parent companies of requiring that local joint venture partners in a developing country subscribe to a gentleman's agreement that the local subsidiary refrain from invading the parent's market preserve in other markets. [37] Robert Cohen analysed how large capital investments in

36 Frank, op. cit.

37 UNCTC, "Transnational corporations and incentives and performance requirements ...".

home country facilities make it difficult to close established plants.[38] Douglas Bennett and Kenneth Sharpe showed that the efforts of organized labour in developed countries to prevent plant closings constitute a drag on the evolution of corporations towards global sourcing.[39] The problem of stickiness in intra-firm trade is not minor. According to the International Monetary Fund, 25 per cent of United States imports of manufactures from developing countries take place between related parties, reaching one third for Brazil and three quarters for Malaysia, Mexico and Singapore.[40] Helleiner argues that TRIMs may be needed to compensate for the bias among affiliates within a single corporation.

Moving from evidence about industry structure to evidence about firm behaviour, what data are there about how transnational corporations respond to TRIMs?

2. *Evidence on corporate responses*

The universe of studies which evaluate the responses of transnational corporations to TRIM requirements is small, consisting of four attempts, three of which were introduced in the preceding chapter. The four are the United States International Trade Commission study of the impact of foreign trade-related performance requirements on United States industry (1982); the World Bank study on incentives and performance requirements by Guisinger and associates (1985); an Overseas Private Investment Corporation study (1987); and a sector-specific study of TRIMs in the petrochemical industry by H. Peter Gray and Ingo Walter (1984).

The principal findings of these four studies regarding the impact of TRIMs are summarized in the following:

a. United States International Trade Commission study

The ITC study of the automotive, chemical and computer and office equipment industries defined TRIMs as export minimums, import maximums

38 Robert B. Cohen, "International investment strategies and domestic reorganization plans of the U.S. automakers: an essay on the response of the U.S. auto firms to changes in international competitiveness in auto production and their impact on the U.S. economy", cited in Douglas C. Bennett and Kenneth E. Sharpe, *Transnational Corporations Versus the State: The Political Economy of the Mexican Auto Industry* (Princeton, N.J., Princeton University Press, 1985), p. 198.

39 Bennett and Sharpe, op. cit., p. 243.

40 Cited in G.K. Helleiner, *Intra-Firm Trade and Developing Countries* (New York, St. Martin's Press, 1981).

and local content rules. The survey results on how many overseas affiliates of United States corporations were operating under TRIM requirements, and on which countries imposed the TRIM requirements, were examined in the preceding chapter. In addition, the firms surveyed were also asked whether the TRIM requirements played a large (or small) role in their investment decisions, and whether the TRIMs stimulated or hindered direct investment. They were also asked to estimate the quantitative impact of TRIM requirements on inter-affiliate trade in the sense of how such trade would be altered by the removal of the TRIMs. The ITC investigators then used an input-output model of the United States Department of Labor to translate the trade changes into variations in employment in the affected industries.

With regard to the automotive industry, the existence of TRIMs was reported most often to be a minor factor in the decision by a United States motor-vehicle manufacturer to invest in a foreign country. United States direct foreign investment expanded slightly due to the use of TRIM requirements abroad because investing firms were required to increase investment for host country production rather than to import certain products. Seven firms indicated that, in the absence of performance requirements, United States trade with their affiliates would have changed, but only four firms could (or would) quantify such changes. These four firms indicated that United States exports would have increased to two countries (Mexico and Brazil) and decreased to two others (Venezuela and Canada) for a net export expansion of $84.7 million (0.9 per cent of the automotive industry respondents' total exports to their affiliates). At the same time, United States imports from two countries, Canada and Mexico, would have decreased by $59.6 million. Based on the estimated loss of exports and increase in imports in the year of the survey, United States production in the motor vehicle equipment industry fell by $144.3 million. This output loss translated into a total job loss of 2,008 positions in the motor vehicle and equipment industry plus industries providing goods and services to that industry. However, three of the four United States motor vehicle manufacturers disputed the reported findings (with particular emphasis on Mexico), indicating that the absence of TRIM requirements would have resulted in lower United States exports. These three firms asserted that the use of TRIM requirements and accompanying investment incentives, particularly market protection, by a host country allowed foreign firms a greater presence in that country than would be the case with an open market. Therefore, they argued, in the absence of TRIM requirements, United States exports to these affiliates would be lost or reduced. Moreover, they pointed out, by encouraging the development of a domestic motor-vehicle industry through the use of TRIMs, a host country creates a market for United States exports of capital goods.

With regard to the chemical industry, the existence of TRIMs was again reported to be a relatively minor factor in the decision by Unites States chemical firms to invest outside the home country. United States direct investment abroad was slightly retarded by the use of TRIM requirements, and would have increased overall by $56.9 million in their absence. Trade flows were affected by performance requirements in that exports from the home country to affiliates of six respondents operating under TRIM requirements were lessened because of those requirements. Four of the respondents quantified this altered pattern of trade, reporting that, in the absence of TRIM requirements, United States exports to eight countries (Brazil, Mexico, Spain, the Republic of Korea, Peru, Indonesia, Colombia and India) would have increased by $74.2 million (1.7 per cent of respondents' total exports to their affiliates) in the year of the survey. This output reduction translated into a total job loss of 605 positions in the chemical sector plus industries providing goods and services to the chemical sector.

With regard to the computer and office equipment industry, TRIMs were once again reported to have had no more than a minor effect on the decision to invest abroad. United States foreign direct investment would have, in the absence of TRIM requirements, declined by $18.3 million in Mexico and $146,000 in Spain and increased by $1.2 million in Brazil, for an overall decrease of $17.2 million. The reported impact of performance requirements on United States trade in the year of the survey was a small decline in exports and a minuscule decrease in imports. Three firms surveyed indicated that, in the absence of TRIM requirements, United States trade with their affiliates would have changed, but only two firms could quantify these changes, reporting that exports would have increased by $13.6 million (0.5 per cent of the sector respondents' total exports to their affiliates). Based on the estimated loss of both United States exports and imports, the United States output decline translated into a total job loss of 341 positions for the entire sector as well as industries providing goods and services to that sector.

In total, the estimated employment loss due to TRIMs in the automotive, chemical and computer and office equipment industries, plus all industries providing goods and services to those sectors, was less than three thousand jobs.

b. The World Bank study [41]

The study by Guisinger and associates for the World Bank attempted to measure the effectiveness of TRIMs imposed on foreign investors by asking the latter to compare their behaviour in a country under actual incentive-and-disincentive policies with a hypothetical outcome in which that country removed its TRIM investment package while the investment packages of all other countries remained constant.

The study found that TRIM requirements did increase exports and reduce imports of intermediate products in the automobile industry. The authors hypothesized that the automobile industry had something of a "footloose" quality about it due to mature production technology. In the computer industry, in contrast, TRIM requirements did not play an important role in changing trade patterns. In the food-processing industry, where 12 of 25 firms were subject to TRIM requirements, performance requirements were calculated to have reduced total foreign investment. In the petrochemical industry, developed countries had a history of heavy subsidies to induce transnational firms to locate near markets, while the use of TRIMs by developing countries was just beginning a process of policy catch-up which had not yet affected firm locations significantly.

Overall, while 38 of the 74 cases in the sample were subject to explicit TRIM requirements (and in some of the other cases the incentive package was tied to trade performance), TRIM requirements were instrumental in altering the location of the investment in only four of the 74 cases. Yet the study team found strong competition for potential foreign investors. In two thirds of the 74 cases surveyed, the decision where to locate the investment was influenced by incentive policies offered by the host Government. At the margin, host Governments could not reduce their packages to attract foreign firms without losing substantial inward investment. Interviews with government officials demonstrated that they had considerable knowledge about what kind of investment packages were offered elsewhere; moreover, the study noted an appreciable follow-the-leader pattern among potential host Governments in the effort to attract foreign firms and influence their operations.

Direct subsidies to affect the location and operations of foreign firms were more common in developed market economies, while trade protection to accomplish the same goal was more frequent in developing countries. The firms reported that front-end cash grants in the European Community con-

41 Guisinger and associates, op. cit.

stituted a great facilitator of the investment decision. France, for example, provided more than 50 per cent of all investment costs in cash to firms willing to locate in regions targeted for "development". In one case in Europe, $500,000 of parent company new money was leveraged, via public grants, into building and equipping a $50 million facility. The evidence from the European Community showed an upward trend over time in the net cash equivalent of investment-incentive packages.

There was a large degree of non-transparent TRIM-like behaviour on the part of countries that did not utilize explicit TRIM requirements. The Industrial Development Authority in Ireland and the Economic Development Board in Singapore were singled out as notable examples where leverage was exercised through discretionary incentive policies. Both agencies rewarded projects designed to meet trade performance objectives and withheld benefits from projects that did not, instead of imposing explicit domestic content and export-minimum requirements. Firms reported that many countries with TRIM requirements on the books, in contrast, did not always enforce them.

In several of the 38 cases subject to TRIM requirements, corporate officials informed the study team that their firms would have eventually achieved the levels of exports or domestic content required by the TRIM regulations on their own. The principal impact of the TRIMs was to accelerate the firms' plans to develop local suppliers and enter export markets. In the automobile industry, corporate officials reported that domestic content regulations might raise local costs but that achieving competitive local supply prices was not an unattainable goal.

c. The Overseas Private Investment Corporation study [42]

The study of a sample of OPIC projects found that, in the great majority of cases (83 per cent), TRIMs did not require investors to alter their patterns of purchases or sales significantly to meet the requirements. In the case of local content requirements, firms typically reported that it was either more economical to source domestically or that the sourcing requirement was negotiable. In the case of export minimums, firms typically reported that it had been their intention from the start to export part or all of their production. The redundancy of the TRIM requirements permitted OPIC to conclude that the TRIMs did not, *per se*, significantly affect the pattern of trade, and therefore did not lower

42 See, Theodore H. Moran and Charles Pearson, *Trade Related Investment Performance Requirements* (Washington, Overseas Private Investment Corporation, 1987).

substantially what positive trade benefits the home country would gain from the investment.

Of the four instances in which the TRIM requirements were considered non-redundant, OPIC concluded that in three cases no significant amount of home country exports would be displaced, and in one case the additional exports of the project to the home country would simply displace imports from other sources.

d. *Trade-related investment measures in the petrochemical industry*[43]

H. Peter Gray and Ingo Walter examined a representative sample of 15 petrochemical projects involving transnational corporations based in the United States, Europe and Japan. They evaluated the operations with corporate planners and headquarters personnel to determine the existence of TRIMs, whether statutory or discretionary; the impact of TRIM measures on project economics; and the effect on plant-location decisions, operating characteristics and trade patterns. Their results are summarized in table 13.

In general they found that corporate strategic thinking dominated firm decision-making with regard to project placement and design, with investment incentives and performance requirements playing a secondary role in choosing among alternative sites from which to pursue the larger corporate objectives. The exception occurred when sub-scale plants for relatively limited national markets required the assurance of ongoing protection from import competition. In selecting locales for large-scale production to supply global markets, there was noticeable competition among the TRIM packages on the part of countries that were near-substitutes (Saudi Arabia vs. Canada, Colombia vs. the Philippines, Canada vs. Trinidad or Indonesia). The authors viewed the establishment of protected plants in small countries relatively benignly on technology-transfer and infant-industry grounds (for a contrary view, see below) and concluded that the use of TRIM packages does not seriously distort the pattern of trade in petrochemicals. In several cases, in fact, they found that export-related TRIMs improved world welfare in comparison to the alternative of non-intervention.

* * * * * * * *

43 H. Peter Gray and Ingo Walter, "Investment-related trade distortions in petrochemicals", *Journal of World Trade Law* (January 1984), pp. 283-307.

Table 13. Survey of the petrochemical industry: significance of investment incentives and performance requirements in investment and/or operating decisions

Case:	*1*	*2*	*3*	*4*	*5*	*6*	*7*	*8*	*9*	*10*	*11*	*12*	*13*	*14*	*15*
Country: Measure	*Canada*	*Saudi Arabia*	*Saudi Arabia*	*Brazil*	*Rep.of Korea*	*Brazil*	*Germany*	*Mexico*	*Mexico*	*Belgium*	*Singa-pore*	*Colombia*	*Sri Lanka*	*Mexico*	*Pakis-tan*
Tax exemption or reduction			..	..	..	..					..				
Tax holidays				..	..						..				..
Accelerated depreciation					..			.		..	..		...		.
Investment tax credits					..				...						
Development zone incentives				..								..	...		
Key industry incentives					...							..			
Excess profit taxes															000
Cash grants							.			..					
Direct subsidies							.								
Concessionary financing		...	...			..					..	.			
Loan guarantees					..										
Preferential access to capital markets				.	..										
Protection against devaluation															..
Ownership limits		00	. 00	0	000	00		0	0			000		00	
Merger limits					000										
Remittance limits			00	00		00		0	0			00	00	00	
Tariff exemptions or reductions			.	..	..	..					.	..			
Tariff exemptions on exports											.				..
Export tax credits				..								..			
Export concessionary financing				..	.	..					.	.			
Export guarantees				..											
Export tax allowance				..							.				
Tariff protection			.	...	...	...		...	...					...	...
Export requirements				0				00	0			000			
Feedstock subsidy		..	...		..			..	.						

Case:	1	2	3	4	5	6	7	8	9	10	11	12	13	14	15
Country: Measure	*Canada*	*Saudi Arabia*	*Saudi Arabia*	*Brazil*	*Rep.of Korea*	*Brazil*	*Germany*	*Mexico*	*Mexico*	*Belgium*	*Singa-pore*	*Colombia*	*Sri Lanka*	*Mexico*	*Pakis-tan*
Energy subsidy			..					.	.						
Wage subsidy			..	.					.	.					
Curtailed strikes					.										
High-quality government trained labour		00											..	..	
Wage controls															
Tax exemptions for expatriates					.										
Job creation					.										
Input tax deductions					.										
Local labour requirement		0	00			0									
Local content requirement			0		00								00		
Management-control limitations	.				000										
Oil entitlements		..	..									00	00	0	0
Research and development			.	.	.										
supports					..										
No government competition										..					
Restricted markets				..	00										000
Environmental tolerance					00										00
Price controls					00	00									
Profit formulas															
Plant site restrictions															
Closed industries															

Source: H. Peter Gray and Ingo Walter, "Investment-related trade distortions in petrochemicals", *Journal of World Trade Law* 18 (January 1984), p. 293.

. Marginally significant incentive.
.. Important incentive.
... Critical incentive.
0 Marginally significant disincentive.
00 Important disincentive.
000 Critical disincentive.

From these four studies, what conclusions can one draw about the impact of TRIMs on investor behaviour? There are three important findings.

- *First*, despite a methodology which biases the potential impact of TRIMs upwards by asking how firms would alter their behaviour if TRIMs were removed in TRIM-using countries but all other locational policies in all other countries remained in place, the reported shifts in firm behaviour due to TRIM regulations are surprisingly small.[44] Foreign investors are not "jerked around" in conspicuous ways as the neo-classical paradigm would suggest. Nor is the international trading system imperilled by the presence of TRIMs. Indeed, as the next chapter will discuss, one might conclude that the representation of TRIMs as being a high priority trade policy issue is not fully supported by the evidence.
- *Second*, however, there is clear evidence of competition among potential host countries to secure foreign direct investment, with developed countries frequently using market access, tariff escalation and investment incentives to attract investors to their jurisdictions, in the same way as developing countries use TRIMs. In this context, developing countries may utilize domestic content and export requirements as part of an effort, at the margin, to offset locational policies at alternative sites. This appears particularly true in "footloose" industries, the term "footloose" being used to characterize industries with multiple alternative comparable-cost production sites, with the Guisinger study providing cases from the automotive industry and the Gray-Walter study providing cases from the petrochemical industry. In the latter industry, TRIMs were used in developing countries in an effort to "catch up" with earlier public policy efforts on the part of developed countries.
- *Third*, is the discovery that TRIMs frequently "require" firms to do what they find to be in their own interest, merely speeding up a process of searching out local suppliers or expanding exports in a way they would eventually do on their own in any event. This finding is compatible with the presence of oligopoly in which firms have discretion about where to locate production and an ability to "satisfice" in their decision-making (settle for less than the optimum

44 This finding is further documented in a Conference Board survey of more than 100 United States, Canadian and European transnational corporations. Fewer than 5 per cent of the companies reported that they had actually altered an investment decision due to TRIMs. *Operating Foreign Subsidiaries* (New York, The Conference Board, 1983).

locale rather than spend extra resources to identify the "perfect" site when it is uncertain whether the cost differential would be worth such expenditure). Similarly, this finding is consistent with the existence of intra-firm rigidities where firms have fixed investments in plant and labour at a given site and prefer not to incur the adjustment costs of exit or the start-up costs of a new untried locale. The evidence here leaves open the possibility for a dynamic infant-industry role for TRIMs, pushing firms to discover novel backward and forward linkages.

What is the actual impact of TRIM regulations on the allocation of resources? Is it beneficial or malign? Except under conditions of perfect competition, this question cannot be answered simply by looking at aggregate levels of firm response. Instead, one must move to the next level of analysis, case studies of TRIM-governed foreign investment projects, to see whether subsidiary operations run parallel or contrary to international comparative advantage, enhancing or retarding the efficient use of resources on local and global levels.

3. *Evidence from case studies*

There is an appalling lack of detailed, careful micro-studies of the impact of TRIMs on the allocation of economic resources within a particular industry or, more broadly, on the allocation of economic resources within the country where a TRIM occurs. Nevertheless, what evidence there is about the economic impact of TRIMs falls into two widely divergent categories of outcome.

a. *Failures of trade-related investment measures*

The first category tends to include some combination of sub-economic size of operation, subsidies to offset the high costs borne by foreign investors and shelter from competition. This results in economic inefficiencies as well as weak stimulus for dynamic gains from technological change or learning-curve advantages for management. Examples include:

- *In the automotive industry*: Harvey Bale and David Walters found 16 countries with less than a 100,000 vehicle output per year where TRIMs requiring from 18 per cent to 100 per cent domestic content have to be supported with *ad valorem* import tariffs which average nearly 100 per cent.[45] In a classic study of one case with near-100 per cent domestic content TRIMs, the Indian automobile industry, Anne Krueger estimated that 27 of 34 assemblers and associated industries in India enjoyed effective rates of protection above 50 per cent at the time of her study, with almost half of the firms receiving more than 100 per cent (the highest, for a metal fabricator, was 642 per cent).[46] If the effective rate of protection could merely have been capped at 50 per cent, the author calculated, value-added in production would have risen by 34 per cent. Instead, increasingly costly and uneconomic results led to increasingly restrictive trade and foreign exchange policies to preserve the uncompetitive plants. A more recent study of the Indian automobile industry shows that the combination of small scale operations combined with high domestic content requirements (30 per cent to 40 per cent) has continued to hinder the export potential of Indo-Japanese joint ventures.[47]

- *In the petrochemical industry*: Gray and Walter found in their study of 15 representative petrochemical projects subject to TRIMs that scale of output was a decisive factor in the economic outcome (usually but not exclusively associated with export orientation).[48] In two of the least successful cases (Republic of Korea and Pakistan), import protection and quasi-monopoly status were not enough to prevent troubled operations, leading to a vicious cycle of ever more intrusive host government interventions. (In the Korean case, the company, Dow Chemical, which had been the country's largest single foreign investor, ultimately sold its holdings and withdrew.)

- *In the computer/informatics industry*: Leaving aside the area of "market reserve" in Brazil (where foreign direct investment was excluded), Claudio Frischtak estimated that foreign computer producers, with large domestic content regulations and high protection, charge two-to-three times as much as rates available outside the country.[49] (IBM disputed this relative price assertion, citing price

45 Harvey E. Bale, Jr., and David Walters, "Investment policy aspects of U.S. and global trade interests", *Looking Ahead*, National Planning Association, 9 (January 1986), pp. 1-14.

46 Anne O. Krueger, *The Benefits and Costs of Import Substitution in India: A Microeconomic Study* (Minneapolis, University of Minnesota Press, 1975).

47 UNCTC "Transnational corporations and incentives and performance requirements in ...".

48 Gray and Walter, op. cit.

49 Claudio Frischtak, "Brazil", in Francis W. Rushing and Carole Ganz Brown, eds., *National Policies for Developing High Tech Industries: International Comparisons* (Boulder, Westview Press, 1986).

controls which lower the amount it can charge.)[50] This reduces the relative use of computers in the Brazilian economy to perhaps one fourth the intensity one might expect by international standards, according to William Cline,[51] producing a drag which hits the high-technology portions of Brazil's economy particularly hard. (Embraer, the state aviation enterprise, for example, has publicly criticized the high cost and scarcity of advanced computer capabilities.)[52] Similarly, in India, fiscal and policy constraints designed to protect the local market have repeatedly hindered transnational firms from expanding computer and other electronics exports despite the professed desire on the part of public authorities to provide access to foreign exchange and duty free inputs for export activities.[53]

One might suspect that import-substitution projects subject to TRIMs are more likely to fall into the category of economic failures than export-oriented projects subject to TRIMs. While this generally appears to be accurate, it should not obscure the fact that basic economic inefficiency can just as easily spoil export-oriented projects as well. Dennis Encarnation and Louis Wells reported on sub-optimally sized metal smelting operations in one country and food processing ventures in another whose net social contributions were negative, given an incentive package which included below market-price energy whose sale on world markets in the form of petroleum would procure more than enough revenue to pay the local participants for doing nothing.[54]

These TRIM failures should remind the analyst that while there may be a positive argument for public sector intervention under conditions of imperfect competition, such intervention can worsen the situation (if carried out improperly) rather than improve it. David Richardson has calculated, for example, that constraints on trade under conditions of imperfect competition can create losses in efficiency two or three times as large as similar constraints under perfect competition.[55]

---

50 William Cline, *Informatics and Development: Trade and Industrial Policy in Argentina, Brazil, and Mexico* (Washington, Economics International, 1987), p. 61.

51 Ibid, pp. 61-63.

52 Ibid., p. 64.

53 UNCTC, "Transnational corporations and incentives and performance requirements ...".

54 Dennis J. Encarnation and Louis T. Wells, Jr., "Evaluating foreign investment", in Theodore H. Moran, *et. al.*, *Investing in Development: New Roles for Private Capital?* (Washington, Overseas Development Council, 1986), pp. 61-86.

55 See Richardson, op. cit.

b. Successes of trade-related investment measures

The second category of outcomes tends to include some combination of economic size of operation (full realization of economies of scale); subsidies to compensate foreign investors for the burden of exit, adjustment and uncertainty; and subsequent exposure of the project to competition. This leads to an efficient use of resources, with positive results from technological change and learning-curve experience, and possible linkages with associated and supplier industries in the domestic economy. Examples include:

- *In the automotive industry*: In Mexico, domestic content TRIMs introduced foreign automobile firms, especially Ford, Volkswagen, Chrysler and Nissan (and, with even less hesitation, foreign automotive parts firms) to the prospect that Mexico could become "an integral part of the strategic sourcing network of its U.S. parent".[56] When Mexico attempted to enforce export TRIMs after 1977, with the threat that non-compliers would have to withdraw from the market, General Motors experienced conflicting internal pressures. On the one hand, GM's sourcing network in the United States was much more embedded within the GM divisions themselves, imposing a heavier burden of intra-firm displacement. On the other hand, General Motors was in the midst of a crisis, needing to reduce costs or continue to lose market share precipitously. Despite opposition from the United Auto Workers in the United States, Mexican authorities ultimately prevailed in influencing GM decision-making. General Motors announced in 1979 its largest one-time investment ever in the simultaneous construction of four engine plants, designed to expand exports from Mexico 20-fold.[57] In follow-the-leader fashion VW, Chrysler, Nissan and Ford announced export expansion projects of similar dimensions in the same year so as to maintain their share of the internal Mexican market. The automotive parts industry followed suit: between 1979 and 1989, United States imports (alone) of automotive equipment from Mexico grew from $1.1 billion to $4.5 billion.[58]

56 Barbara C. Samuels II, *Managing Risk in Developing Countries: National Demands and Multinational Response* (Princeton, Princeton University Press, 1990), p. 145. See also Bennett and Sharpe, op. cit.

57 Samuels, op. cit., p. 153.

58 Bennett and Sharpe, op. cit., table 10.2, updated with data from the United States Department of Commerce, 1990.

- *In the petrochemical industry*: The Gray-Walter survey includes three projects (an agro-chemical project in Colombia and two feedstock/intermediate projects in Saudi Arabia) which demonstrate an effective use of TRIMs. In Colombia, authorities granted 100 per cent foreign ownership, export tax credits and expedited approval for land and capacity expansion in return for an 80 per cent export commitment, winning the contract (over the Philippines). In the Saudi cases, the Government subsidized unusually large infrastructure expenses to bring capital costs in line with those more common elsewhere (e.g., Canada), while supplying feedstock from abundant and underutilized natural gas at a favourably low price. Gray and Walter calculated that, without the beneficial TRIM package, the investors would not have chosen Saudi Arabia for world production, but with the favourable TRIM package, global welfare and global resource allocation were improved (since the probable alternative disposal of the natural gas would be flaring).
- *In the computer/informatics industry*: It is improbable that Mexico's early domestic content TRIMs in the computer industry induced foreign companies into contemplating the use of a Mexican site for global production, given the extreme disincentive from a 51 per cent national ownership requirement. When Mexico refocused its TRIM strategy after 1985 on export performance in return for a relaxation of the historical joint-ownership provision, the Government induced IBM to consider a world-scale sized export facility: IBM's original investment offer had been $7 million; the subsequent proposal for a facility whose output was more than 90 per cent destined for export was $91 million. In reaction, Wilson Perez Nuñez points out, Apple and Hewlett Packard reversed their own earlier strategies of producing high-cost products exclusively for the protected local market, and offered to meet a three-to-one export/import ratio in return for 100 per cent ownership.[59]

These TRIM success stories fit the scenario (highlighted earlier in the discussion of strategic trade) in which a fear-of-loss coupled with a promise-of-gain can propel a transnational corporation out of a sticky pattern of operations. The TRIMs then "establish" the nation as one host among several alternative production sites in an industry with large economies of scale.

* * * * * * * *

59 Wilson Perez Nuñez, *Foreign Investment and Industrial Development in Mexico* (Paris, OECD Development Centre, 1990). See also Cline, *Informatics and Development*, op. cit.

This micro-analysis of TRIM successes and failures does not suggest that scale factors are the sole determinant of one outcome or the other. Nor does it demonstrate that, even in the successful cases, the same outcome could not be achieved more readily with another policy tool rather than a TRIM. (For the advantages and disadvantages of TRIMs as a public policy tool, see chapter III). It does suggest, however, that under conditions of imperfect competition there may be a need for public sector intervention and that TRIMs may be one way of carrying out such intervention effectively.

Given the wide divergence of outcomes, one cannot be complacent about advocating a general usage of TRIMs. There is no substitute for a careful examination of industry structure and TRIM design, nor for exacting micro-level analysis of the project to see whether the effort makes economic sense. As the final chapter will argue, Governments in developing countries (using TRIMs backed by trade-rents from consumers) have the same responsibility as authorities in Ireland, Spain or the state of Tennessee (using subsidies financed by taxes on constituents) to scrutinize each proposed project to determine whether the outcome will be a waste of scarce resources.

C. Summary of theory and evidence on the impact of trade-related investment measures

This chapter showed that the impact one can expect TRIMs to have on trade and development depends centrally on the context in which they are employed. Within a neo-classical context of perfect competition, TRIMs misallocate resources and hurt the welfare even of the country which employs them. Within a strategic trade context of imperfect competition, on the other hand, TRIMs may play a positive role in stimulating development and compensating for distortions in trade, enhancing home country welfare and (perhaps) global welfare as well. One must not conclude, of course, that they automatically have such a positive impact. (Even with imperfect competition, TRIMs may simply represent a particularly clumsy effort at import substitution.) But at their best, they could serve as a neo-infant-industry stimulus, especially where, on the one hand, there are increasing returns to scale and dynamic gains from learning by doing and, on the other hand, stickiness in firm response due to large fixed investments in plant and human capital elsewhere, high exit costs (including delicate relations with organized labour) and risk aversion to uncertainty about the gains from relocation.

Turning from theory to evidence, there is a preponderance of data suggesting that industries in which foreign direct investment takes place are not perfectly competitive, with oligopoly figuring prominently in both international and domestic markets where TRIMs are located. This implies that transnational firms do have discretion about where to locate. And they do exhibit some of the stickiness indicated above. At the level of firm response to TRIMs, the data reveal a surprisingly small level of change in firm behaviour attributable to TRIMs. In part, this was due to the firms reporting that they intended to build up local supplier networks or develop external markets which the domestic content and export TRIMs required them to do anyway. In part, this may be due to the firms' own bargaining power in resisting host country TRIM demands. In either case, the consistent discovery of very limited alterations in firm behaviour suggests that the contemporary worry that TRIMs force investors to act in a manner which undermines the global trading system is exaggerated. At the same time, however, the data reveal considerable competition among potential host sites, with authorities fearing that any contestant who does not offer an appealing locational package and nail down investor commitments will be left behind.

A further level of analysis is needed to determine whether TRIM packages themselves do or do not enhance efficiency in the use of resources. For that, one must examine individual projects at the micro level. Here, the evidence seems to cluster at two extremes. At one end, there are TRIM-governed projects which are failures in enhancing host country development or international comparative advantage. These are associated with sub-optimal economic size and shelter from competition, with implicit or explicit subsidies to make up for (permanently) high costs. At the other end, there are TRIM-governed projects which are successes in enhancing the use of resources in the host country and abroad. These are associated with a full utilization of economies of scale and ultimate subjection of the project to competition, with implicit and explicit subsidies aimed at overcoming corporate reluctance to bear transitional relocation/redesign costs and uncertainties. This dichotomy tends to confirm the idea in both the neo-classical and strategic trade literature that public sector intervention is helpful if it provides all roughly comparable sites with an equal chance to harness foreign investment for global markets, but unhelpful if it merely shelters high-cost facilities from competition.

Overall, the analysis in this chapter suggests that, under conditions of imperfect competition, there may be a need for public sector intervention, and that TRIMs can be one means to carry out such intervention effectively. But TRIMs in and by themselves do not ensure a beneficial outcome and, even when they are successful, there may be other policy tools which would achieve the same outcome more readily. Moreover, if imperfect competition justifies intervention for one set of authorities, it offers equal justification for others.

The result, as this chapter warned, could be that all end up worse off than they would be if they could arrange to exercise mutual restraint.

These are issues (the advantages and disadvantages of TRIMs in comparison to alternative methods of achieving the same result, and the need to limit competition in offering favourable locational packages) which will be dealt with in the final chapter.

III. Conclusions and policy implications

Over the past decade, economic analysis has begun a cautious reassessment of public policy designed to affect international patterns of industrial activity. This reassessment has underscored new findings, for example, that public authorities cannot depend upon discovering atomistic competition in markets where international investment takes place, and that governmental intervention may be justified to correct for market failure. It has also reiterated old lessons, for example, that sheltering firms from competition is highly costly, and that trade protection carries perhaps the greatest shelter a firm can enjoy. The reassessment has not simplified the design of public policy; on the contrary, it has complicated the task and shown the process to be fraught with dangers.

In general, this reconsideration has limited itself to the analysis of economic strategy for developed countries. Only slowly have parallel forms of analysis been extended to cover the equally fruitful terrain of developing country policies. As this study has shown, the major structural characteristics which inspired the reconsideration of policies for the developed countries are present in the economic environment of the developing countries as well. The issues have the same relevance, the dilemmas the same poignancy. Indeed, as developing countries search for ways to expand their economies with a broader play of market forces than has prevailed in the past, the debate about the scope of legitimate public action to influence the location and composition of production takes on growing relevance.

Yet, the area in which North-South tensions about what constitutes legitimate public action is most keenly felt, namely, the debate about employing TRIMs to support developmental or commercial goals, remains untouched by the subtlety of this reassessment. In the TRIMs debate, a certain dogmatism prevails, to the effect that public sector intervention is by definition distortionary and deserving of peremptory condemnation by responsible policy makers.

If the stakes were purely intellectual, there might be less overwhelming reason to be concerned. But the stakes also involve very real economic costs, with results potentially disadvantageous to the efforts of developing countries to expand trade and development (and, one must add, with results possibly detrimental to global economic welfare, including the welfare of developed countries as well).

What is the role of TRIMs as a tool for development and trade strategy, and how can policies of developed and developing countries be harmonized multilaterally to minimize the conflict over TRIMs and maximize the economic gains for all countries?

A. Trade-related investment measures and development policy

When the question of the relationship between TRIMs and development policy is posed within the neo-classical paradigm of perfect competition, the analysis is relatively straightforward and simple. The basic argument was spelled out in chapter I: TRIMs within a neo-classical context mean inefficiency and a hindrance to growth.

The evidence in this study has shifted the framework for analysis away from the neo-classical paradigm towards a focus on imperfect markets, both globally and in the host country, for those industries in which foreign direct investment takes place. The presence of oligopoly complicates the analysis of appropriate policies greatly, and renders outcomes much more problematic; but it does not lead the policy debate towards passivity. When dealing with international oligopoly, public authorities can err as much by sins of omission as by sins of commission.

How do TRIMs fit into a development strategy which must cope with imperfect competition in the industries in which foreign investors participate?

1. Domestic content requirements

The traditional justification for domestic content TRIMs is a variant on the standard infant-industry argument, namely, that they provide the learning-curve experience necessary to nurture foreign subsidiaries into becoming world-class producers. As earlier parts of this study have pointed out, however, following a learning curve along a path of operating a sub-economic-sized plant for a market protected from imports offers a disadvantaged educational experience. To be fair, however, the automotive-parts subsidiaries of foreign firms, after all, pushed the idea of global sourcing from Mexico early even though their initial operations had been structured to satisfy domestic content TRIMs.[60]

A further justification for domestic content TRIMs is the consideration in chapter II of situations where the monopsonistic power of foreign subsidiaries (which produce final products) drives down the price to competitive local suppliers, leading to underconsumption of domestic components. A local content TRIM requirement can correct this foreign investor-induced distortion, raising host country welfare.[61]

The development strategist will want to note several complications, however.

- *First,* a production subsidy for local component production would be more direct, and hence perhaps preferable, to a domestic content TRIM.
- *Second,* the actual circumstances surrounding any particular case could be less clear-cut than the highly stylized model of the "optimal" domestic content TRIM:
  - If locally produced input costs cannot be made comparable to the price of imported components even when scale economies are achieved and learning-curve advantages fully realized, the "optimal" domestic content TRIM will not produce the desired results;[62]
  - If foreign final goods-producing subsidiaries and domestic final goods-producing firms are granted very high protection (via an import quota or a prohibitive tariff), the decline in consumer surplus may outweigh a shift in producer surplus, leaving a negative net impact on host country welfare;[63]
  - If the local suppliers to the foreign final goods-producing subsidiaries are themselves imperfectly competitive, the bargaining outcome between oligopsonistic final goods producers and oli-

60 As one Volkswagen executive expressed it, as the requirement for domestic content rose "one way to stop cost increases was to export more". Samuels, op. cit., p. 146.

61 Martin Richardson, op. cit. See also the work by Vousden and Krishna and Itoh, op. cit.

62 Martin Richardson's model depends on an assumption of comparable costs.

63 Carl Davidson, Stephen J. Matusz and Mordechai E. Kreinen include the assumption of infinite protection in their model and predict a negative outcome. See their "Analysis of performance standards for direct foreign investments", *Canadian Journal of Economics*, vol. 18 (November 1985), pp. 876-890.

gopolistic component suppliers becomes indeterminate and the net welfare effects unclear;

— If local suppliers are imperfectly competitive, the distributional implications for the host country society become less appealing as domestic oligopolists (and privileged labour) gain at the expense of local consumers;

— Finally, if local suppliers are imperfectly competitive and include foreign subsidiaries, the mixture of benefits captured by domestic oligopolists, foreign oligopolists, and the host country labour elite becomes even more complicated.

Thus, domestic content TRIMs could be a legitimate, beneficial tool for development policy, but only in relatively narrow circumstances and as part of very subtle policy formulations. The widespread use of domestic content TRIMs as a device for import substitution, in contrast, like other protectionist policies, carries substantial costs and dangers. In the everyday world of promoting development efforts, the development strategist will probably want to be quite circumspect in advocating the use of domestic content TRIMs.

2. *Export-performance requirements*

Export-performance TRIMs, on the contrary, offer more favourable prospects for promoting host country development if they are utilized as part of an effort to attract industries that have increasing returns to scale and dynamic learning-by-doing effects. One might begin by recalling the strategic trade argument introduced in chapter II: in such industries, only a handful of sites may supply large portions of the global market. The successful inducement of a transnational corporation to locate a world-scale sized facility in a given country bestows large producer surpluses upon that country, embodied in higher earnings for sub-marginal workers and suppliers if the country hosts the operation than if it does not (equal to the area ABE in figure B-1, appendix B). To obtain the foreign direct investment, it is worth paying a handsome price (up to the entire area bounded by ABCD in figure B-1). Moreover, the successful establishment of final goods-production facilities may well give rise to backward and forward linkages in traded and non-traded intermediate goods which also enjoy increasing returns to scale. These Helpman-Krugman "industrial complexes" offer great potential for export-led growth via the harnessing of foreign investors.

The most direct policy to influence a transnational firm to establish a facility in a target locale would be to offer a production subsidy (up to the amount indicated by ABCD in figure B-1). Such a production subsidy could be raised by taxing the population at large, or particular sectors of it.

An alternative approach, however, would be an export or trade-balancing TRIM, offering, say, access to a protected local market in exchange for exports of a certain amount, with total production large enough to capture the relevant economies of scale. (Besides the impact on foreign investor behaviour, an export TRIM can have the added benefit, as Rodrik has pointed out, of shifting producer surplus to indigenous final product producers.[64] In the Rodrik model, the parent corporation reduces output one-for-one as its developing-country subsidiary increases exports while local final product firms fill in extra domestic sales relinquished by the foreign subsidiary as the latter exports.) The disadvantage of export or trade-balancing TRIMs is that they impose the burden of the inducement fee solely on local consumers of the product rather than on taxpayers at large. (Local consumers pay higher prices and suffer lower output while the foreign investor collects trade rents.)

Given this drawback, why might development strategists choose to use export or trade-balancing TRIMs rather than production subsidies?

For most developing countries, a government grant of sufficient size to induce the desired alteration in the behaviour of foreign firms ($120 million to $325 million as recorded for the automobile industry) may simply not be available.[65] Politically speaking, an approach which relied on massive production or export subsidies to foreign firms may not be feasible if it takes an explicit on-budget form. A trade-balancing TRIM, on the other hand, would avoid some of these disadvantages, since a policy of denying market access to a transnational firm which does not comply with the export requirement could be carried out by shifting the local market share to one which did without on-budget costs (the shift itself would involve some adjustment costs). The principal difference, however, lies in the choice between using revenues from taxpayers to provide highly visible subsidies to foreign transnational corpora-

64 Rodrik, op. cit. Using a competitive model, in contrast, Herander and Thomas find that export and export-linkage TRIMs may actually worsen the balance of trade. Their finding depends upon circumstances in which a firm finds it very costly to cut local sales. See Mark G. Herander and Christopher R. Thomas, "Export performance and export-import linkage requirements", *The Quarterly Journal of Economics*, 101 (August 1986), pp. 591-607.

65 One can always argue, of course, that with perfect financial markets the host Government should be able to borrow the necessary funds and, even after discounting the gains, pay the loans back with surplus left over. While this argument is not absurd (e.g., private capital markets will lend funds to Governments of the Republic of Korea and Singapore for infrastructure designed to benefit foreign investors), this option appears limited in most cases.

corporations, and burdening consumers with high prices which transfer rents in less ostentatious fashion to the foreign firms.

In addition, an export-performance TRIM offers the developing country the advantage of receiving a clear *quid pro quo* for the investor's ability to enjoy the protected market. A fiscal incentive which does no more than raise the foreigners' profits could, as the Brecher-Diaz Alejandro analysis revealed (see chapter II), merely allow the parent to siphon off local capital.[66] TRIMs enable the host country to intervene in a focused fashion rather than being a passive provider of benefits. On the political side, a specific *quid pro quo* might be needed to justify the special treatment afforded the foreign corporation. TRIMs may be less open to local criticism and reproach than straight subsidies to foreign investors. Local authorities will be better able to defend themselves by pointing to what they received in return.

The TRIM approach provides a conditionality which may be valuable *vis-à-vis* transnational firms that are reluctant to alter patters of intra-firm trade based on installed capacity. The dual impact of threat-of-loss and promise-of gain may be needed to overcome the rigidities caused by high exit costs and buttressed by aversion to risk.[67] As Raymond Vernon argued, one of the most difficult problems faced by a transnational corporation is to make a plausible estimate of the costs and benefits of a potential investment decision: any such attempt "may be subject to so much inescapable error as to expose the prospective investor to Arrow's well-known dilemma: the firm can't know which course to take until after it's taken it"; in such circumstances, Vernon concluded, policy measures that include threat-of-loss as well as promise-of-gain may be particularly effective.[68]

Finally, the presence of TRIMs as part of the regulations governing foreign investment offer the host the possibility of behaving as a discriminating monopolist, conceding a requirement of great discomfort to the foreign firm for the promise of actions of great value to the local economy. The

66 Brecher and Diaz Alejandro, op. cit.

67 Again, with perfect financial markets, one can argue that there should be no such phenomenon as intra-firm rigidity to take advantage of internal economies of scale. After discounting the stream of added benefits from relocating, the management would want to borrow the funds to make the necessary adjustments. Were this true, the "stickiness" argument would hinge on the firm's willingness to tolerate added risk and uncertainty as opposed to remaining with a known source of profits since, with imperfect competition, the firm would not be driven by the market to alter its behaviour. The costs of discovering a new and cheaper site would be entirely borne by the first investors, while the subsequent gains would be shared by all firms who located there.

68 Correspondence from Raymond Vernon on an earlier draft of this study, 18 October 1990.

IBM-Mexico computer case illustrates this tactic, where the Mexican negotiators abandoned the traditional insistence on joint ownership in order to obtain a large-scale export facility in place of IBM's opening proposal for a domestically oriented plant. At the same time, the existence of TRIM regulations offered a handy tool to engage in what has been called the "obsolescing bargain": restructuring the terms of an investment agreement after the investment has been put in place.[69]

There are technical hurdles in designing an "optimal" export-performance TRIM. One whose impact approximates a per-unit production subsidy would probably be more effective than a lump sum of trade rents in return for a given amount of exports. For any trade-balancing TRIM, a policy which leaves to the firm the decision what exactly to import without tariff and what exactly to export, is most desirable: this approach allows the foreign subsidiary to combine inputs and to export products or sub-products most in line with comparative advantage, encouraging the expansion of those intra-industry and inter-industry linkages that also enjoy increasing returns to scale.

On balance, however, even the most carefully designed export-performance TRIMs are second-best policies to deal with the second-best world of imperfect competition in transnational markets. As in the case of domestic content TRIMs, straightforward production subsidies would be more effective. Nevertheless, to the extent that they are the only feasible tool available to authorities in developing countries in a world in which other Governments are pursuing alternative production-shifting strategies of their own, export performance TRIMs may provide important policy options. To abandon them unilaterally without parallel constraints on the part of others may be a dereliction of duty in the pursuit of host country development.

B. Trade-related investment measures and trade policy

1. *Trade-related investment measures and the debate about trade distortion*

A central question running through the debate about the use of TRIMs is whether TRIMs distort trade flows. This study has made it clear that central

69 For the idea of the "obsolescing bargain", see Raymond Vernon, *Sovereignty at Bay: The Multinational Spread of U.S. Enterprises* (New York, Basic Books, 1971); Theodore H. Moran, ed., *Multinational Corporations: The Political Economy of Foreign Direct Investment* (Lexington, Mass, D.C. Heath, 1985).

to answering the question of distortion is the further question: compared to what?

Conventional discussions of TRIMs enshrine the neo-classical paradigm: the implicit comparison is to a situation in which competitive international markets allocate factors of production with perfect efficiency. In such a comparison, and without further analysis, one can confidently assert that domestic content and export-performance TRIMs are distortionary *per se* (as are all other forms of public intervention to alter production locations and/or trade flows).

Once one moves away from the neo-classical paradigm, the design of appropriate public policy becomes more difficult.

- *First*, public intervention may in fact be needed to correct for market failures, loosen corporate rigidities and improve economic efficiency. Whether such welfare improvements will result is not, of course, certain. But it is important *not* to dismiss out of hand public efforts to influence the composition of economic activity and the pattern of trade, including the possible utilization of TRIMs, as being unquestionably distortionary.
- *Second*, as strategic trade theory demonstrates, every Government will find the attempt to attract "footloose" industries with large-scale economies and important benefits from learning-by-doing in its own interest. Authorities who pass up this opportunity for ideological reasons will find themselves worse off.
- *Third*, however, as strategic trade theory warns, for each Government to pursue its own interest will leave all others worse off (while transnational firms benefit from the competition). After revealing the allure of self-interested intervention, strategic trade theory shows that ultimately there is no beneficial solution without some form of collective action.

Within this context, the question of whether TRIMs are distortionary becomes much more complex. TRIMs are set in the midst of a struggle in both developed and developing countries to influence where production takes place and what trade patterns result as industries become more globalized. (Indeed TRIMs are a comparatively small part of that struggle, as chapter I showed.) To focus on only a single type of locational policies (TRIMs), while leaving comparable policies elsewhere untouched, is not a recipe for eliminating distortion in trade flows.

To make genuine progress towards an economically rational trading system, one must pursue a balanced approach in which the regulation of public policy efforts aimed at influencing investment decisions is carried out in tandem with the regulation of public policy efforts aimed at influencing trade flows. This is where the conventional debate about TRIMs and trade policy has been sorely deficient. Little attention has been devoted to any systematic attempt to integrate consideration of domestic content and export-performance TRIMs with other locational policies.

To accomplish this task one must compare the impact of TRIMs backed by trade protection with the impact of alternative policies to alter the location of productive facilities backed by fiscal incentives. This is no mean feat. Recent studies, however, have shown how such comparisons can be carried out with analytic rigour (see appendix C).

There has been a long debate about the role incentives play in stimulating international investment. In a seminal work, Grant Reuber *et al.* found that 10 of 69 firms surveyed reported that incentives made little or no difference to whether the project was undertaken or not.[70] On this basis, the Reuber study argued: "it is evident that incentives are of some importance, particularly those provided via trade policy and tax measures. On the other hand, most firms are acutely aware of the difficulties posed by such incentives and frequently assert that they are reluctant to undertake projects that are heavily dependent for their success upon the incentives provided by the host country."[71] This has led some analysts to conclude rather broadly that "incentives are generally not significant determinants of DFI flows into LDCs".[72]

On the other hand, in the more recent study examined earlier in chapter II, Guisinger *et al.* posed the counterfactual question to 74 project managers: if instead of the incentive package you have received (or expect to receive for investments in process) the host Government were to offer you no incentives, would your investment decision have been different? In response, 50 of the 74 investors in the Guisinger study indicated that they would have abandoned the project, relocated the project or served the market through exports in the absence of the incentive package. However, some commentators, such as

70 Grant Reuber *et al.*, *Private Foreign Investment in Development* (Oxford, Clarendon Press, 1973).

71 Ibid., p. 128.

72 See Udom Kerdpibule and E. D. Ramstetter, "Foreign investment theories and policy issues", in Seiji Naya, V. Vichit-Vadakan and Udom Kerdpibule, eds., *Direct Foreign Investment and Export Promotion: Policies and Experiences of Asia* (Honolulu, East-West Center, Resource Systems Institute, 1987), p. 11.

Trevor Farrell, have concluded that the findings of the Guisinger group are unusual and different from most previously accepted research.[73]

Louis T. Wells, Jr., has provided an important reinterpretation of the Guisinger data which reconciles it with the apparently contradictory findings of others, including Reuber, and renders the entire body of research highly useful for the present study of TRIMs.[74] He divided the projects into two groups, those whose output was destined exclusively for a small domestic market and those whose output was destined for a large world-scale market. The key difference is whether the investor is focusing on capturing all the economies of scale in production. He then separated the locational inducements, following Guisinger, into "commodity incentives" (tariff protection) and "factor incentives" (fiscal benefits like tax holidays). The results are summarized in table 14.

What Wells found was that, for projects oriented exclusively towards a small domestic market, tariff protection is highly important but fiscal incentives are not, whereas for projects oriented towards large world-scale markets, fiscal incentives are highly important but tariff protection is not. Wells argued that this reconciles Guisinger's work with other surveys, e.g., studies that show that tax incentives in Puerto Rico have a significant impact on international investors who want to supply the United States market.

This sets the stage for the technical analysis in appendix C. There, the examination of recent work by Guisinger shows how the amount of effective protection (the augmentation of value-added in a particular sector due to trade restrictions) and the extent of fiscal incentives (cash grants and tax breaks) interact, in comparable ways, to affect the potential investor's after-tax rate of return.[75]

From the analysis in appendix C, two conclusions are evident:

- *First*, that there is an underlying equivalency between TRIMs and fiscal subsidies in their impact on the profit calculations of transnational investors as they choose where to locate plants.

73 Trevor Farrell, "Incentives and foreign investment decisions: an opposing view", *The CTC Reporter*, 20 (Autumn 1985), p. 39.

74 Louis T. Wells, Jr., "Investment incentives: an unnecessary debate", *The CTC Reporter*, 22 (Autumn 1986), p. 58.

75 Stephen Guisinger, "Total protection: a new measure of the impact of Government interventions on investment profitability", *Journal of International Business Studies*, vol. 20 (Summer 1989), pp. 280-295.

Table 14. Number of investments, by type of incentive that influenced location and by market orientation of project (two categories)

Market orientation of the project	*Type of incentive that influenced location*	
	Commodity (tariff protection)	*Factor (tax holidays, etc.)*
Small domestic markets	23 a/	2
Large world-scale markets	1	15

Source: Louis T. Wells, Jr., derived the above calculation from tables 1-6, Stephen E. Guisiner and associates, *Investment Incentives and Performance Requirements* (New York, Praeger, 1985), p. 49. Projects designed to serve a common market and those for world-wide export were combined into the large world-scale markets category. Wells divided the market orientation of the projects into "domestic" and "export". Wells' use of "domestic" and "export" categories, which may be confusing since some domestic markets could be large enough for world-scale size operations (the United States, Germany, Japan), was replaced with "small domestic markets" and "large world-scale markets" to capture the crucial distinction. See Louis T. Wells, Jr. "Investment incentives: an unnecessary debate", *The CTC Reporter*, 22 (Autumn 1986), p. 58.

a/ Indicates that for 23 of the 41 projects examined, tariff protection was among the top three factors influencing the investment decision.

- *Second*, that developed countries (which utilize fiscal measures more extensively) are already vying vigorously to influence investment decisions in competition with developing countries (which utilize TRIMs more extensively).

As shown in figure C-1 in appendix C, a rate of effective protection of 15 per cent, combined with a 50 per cent cash grant, provides a net incentive — labelled by Guisinger the "rate of total protection" — totalling 33 per cent (the grant adds 18 per cent effective protection). In point of fact, both the cash grant and the rate of net effective protection used in this illustrative example are lower than the figures currently available to investors in the European Community.

In the European Community, Governments can make cash grants of up to 60 per cent of the cost of investment in priority sectors, which already enjoy an average effective rate of protection of 19 per cent. Thus, by Guisinger's measurement, the total rate of protection in the European Community can run as high as 47 per cent. Then, once the project is on-line, manufacturing firms receive a corporate tax rate reduced to 10 per cent in place of the statutory rate of 50 per cent; they are awarded accelerated depreciation on their assets (which are permitted to have a valuation at original cost instead of being required to subtract the amount of the grants received); they receive sizeable worker training grants; and they are eligible to lease assets at subsidized rates.[76] It is not surprising, therefore, that the Guisinger study reported on firms which singled out Ireland as being particularly generous in offering up-front grants for world-scale sized operations.[77] And Gray and Walter pointed out that one of their two European petrochemical cases, in Belgium, would not have been viable without a "backward-area" investment package.[78] In the United States, authorities in more than 24 states offer substantial grants and grant-equivalents to attract world-scale sized industrial investments, with the amount per job rising. Michigan offered $120 million in state and local incentives to attract Mazda in 1984 ($14,000 per job); Indiana offered $110 million to Subaru-Isuzu in 1986 ($51,000 per job); Kentucky offered $325 million to Toyota in 1989 ($108,000 per job).[79]

The overlap with export performance TRIMs is particularly evident when trade patterns are visibly altered. In the Irish case, for example, fiscal benefits are conditional on the size of the operation or the number of jobs created while the small domestic market ensures that most of the output will be exported.[80] The most detailed study using the Guisinger model has found that the switch to investment incentives after Ireland's entry into the European Community left the effective rate of protection to manufacturers unchanged despite the ostensible cuts in tariffs. Even within a large country like the United States, however, the Federal Reserve Bank of St. Louis has documented a positive correlation between the investment promotion expenditures of individual states and the subsequent exports from those states.[81] To say that such investment packages are not "trade related" is hardly an accurate characterization.

---

76 Stephen Guisinger, "Investment related measures", in M.W. Finger and A. Olechowski, eds., *Handbook on Multilateral Trade Negotiations* (Washington, The World Bank, 1987).

77 Guisinger and associates, op. cit.

78 Gray and Walter, op. cit., p. 309.

79 Richard Child Hill, Michael Indergaard and Kunico Fujita, "Flat Rock, home of Mazda: the social impact of a Japanese company on an American community" (Department of Sociology, Michigan State University, 1988), mimeo; "Indiana refuses to pay U.S. $24 million in transplant aid", *Ward's Automotive International*, 5 (May 1990), "Did Kentucky overpay for Toyota?", *Automotive News*, 31 July 1989.

80 Eric Bond and Stephen Guisinger, "Investment incentives as tariff substitutes: a comprehensive measure of protection", *Review of Economics and Statistics*, 67 (February 1985), pp. 91-97.

81 Cletus C. Coughlin, "The competitive nature of state spending on the promotion of manufacturing exports", Review of Federal Reserve Bank of St. Louis, 10 (May/June 1988).

Less evident, but no less real, are cases where governmental efforts to attract foreign direct investment displace subsequent product flows much like domestic content TRIMs would: both embody an element of import substitution. Taken together, United States state outlays to attract inward investment and to promote exports have grown on average by more than 600 per cent between 1976 and 1986.[82]

In this context, a narrow focus on TRIMs as a determinant of investment behaviour is flawed, if one is truly concerned about distortions in patterns of international trade.

2. *Trade-related investment measures and the Uruguay Round negotiations*

The underlying equivalence between fiscal and trade incentives means that both will have to be made subject to a common regime to avoid distortions in international patterns of economic activity. Instead of a comprehensive approach to locational policies, however, the Uruguay Round singled out TRIMs as a special target for reprobation (see appendix A for a more detailed discussion of the negotiations).

One cannot predict the final outcome of the negotiations. But the following observations can be made:

- *First*, the exclusive focus on TRIMs is itself distortionary because it attempts to restrain one kind of locational policy without similar restraints on equivalent locational policies.
- *Second*, the effort to restrain TRIMs may have the effect of shifting negotiations over investment commitments and public incentives from open to closed settings. A decline in transparency would itself be damaging.
- *Third*, a concerted effort to suppress TRIMs (regardless of the outcome) tends to blind authorities to the basic problem of competition for plant sites, jobs and trade advantages. The opportunity for multilateral regulation of this broader competition may be lost in the pursuit of such a one-sided objective.

Thus, beyond the Uruguay Round, further work remains to be done. An alternative that combines the objectives of fairness and efficiency would be to amalgamate the issues of investment treatment, trade incentives and subsidies

82 Ibid.

in a single agreement about locational policies. Within the GATT framework, the subsidies code is, perhaps, the most obvious candidate for further negotiation.

Adding to the complexity of the task is a need to address sub-regional locational efforts (e.g., state or provincial and regional development policies) along with national ones. Studies of the Uruguay Round and beyond come to the same conclusion: "sub-federal and parastatal subsidies must be subject to [subsidies] code disciplines." [83] This will raise numerous objections, of course. It will be a difficult task within the United States to subject the investment promotion of roughly half of the states to multilateral GATT discipline (although in one recent Governor's race in Indiana, the winner campaigned successfully on a platform of denouncing the incentive arrangements given to foreigners as too costly in relation to the benefits for the state). [84] There is evidence of reluctance on the part of some European countries to curtail their options for granting regional investment incentives as they face the reconstruction of the eastern part of Germany, as well as of Eastern Europe. At the end of the day, however, the rivalry among alternative host authorities will hurt them all: they will find what the Federal Reserve Bank of St. Louis has documented for the United States: a competitive interaction in which exports from any one state are negatively affected by promotional expenditures on the part of their neighbours. [85]

Should the negative impact of this rivalry to attract investment become more apparent, those developing countries that have established new controls over industrial subsidies in their own markets (e.g., Argentina, Bolivia, Brazil, Chile and Mexico) might join with developed countries to institutionalize such restraint multilaterally.

Despite the practical difficulties, however, it is necessary to understand the true dimensions of the international challenge (of which TRIMs are merely a part) and have a clear vision of what is required, at least in principle, to meet it. Partial or ad hoc approaches that seek to impose international discipline on selected problem areas, in isolation from others, are bound to fall short of the global dimensions of this challenge. A more comprehensive approach that addresses the interests of host countries as well as of home countries and transnational corporations, in a balanced framework of rights and obligations,

---

83 Gary C. Hufbauer, "Subsidies: race to the finish line" (Washington, D.C., Institute for International Economics, 1990), mimeo., p. 21.

84 "Indiana refuses to pay U.S. $24 million in transplant aid", *Ward's Automotive International*, 5 (May 1990).

85 Coughlin, op. cit.

offers greater possibilities for resolving conflicts over investment policies and investor behaviour. Such an approach has in fact been pursued for some years by the United Nations Commission on Transnational Corporations, in the negotiations on a Code of Conduct on Transnational Corporations.[86] The alternative to establishing such a global regime for foreign direct investment is to drift closer towards what has been called, in an earlier context, "investment wars" over the location of global facilities.[87]

86 For the text of the draft Code see letter dated 31 May 1990 from the Chairman of the Reconvened Special Session of the Commission on Transnational Corporations to the President of the Economic and Social Council (E/1990/94 dated 12 June 1990).

87 C. Fred Bergsten, "Coming investment wars", *Foreign Affairs* (Fall 1974), pp. 135-152.

Appendix A

The Uruguay Round negotiations on trade-related investment measures

A. Pre-Uruguay Round efforts

Multilateral efforts to deal with the issue of foreign direct investment go back to the United Nations Conference on Trade and Employment, held at Havana in 1948. The Final Act of the Conference included the encouragement of the international flow of capital for productive investment as one of the objectives of the proposed International Trade Organization (Article 1:2). [1] Recognition was given in Article 12:1(a) to the fact that international investment "can be of great value in promoting economic development". [2] While the Act suggested that Member States should "give due regard to the desirability of avoiding discrimination as between foreign investments", it was recognized that any State, in so far as other agreements may permit, "might determine whether and to what extent and upon what terms it will allow foreign direct investment", and that "it might take any appropriate safeguards necessary to ensure that foreign investment is not used as a basis for interference in its internal affairs or national policies"; it was also recognized that States may "prescribe and give effect on just terms to requirements as to the ownership of existing and future investment" and to "other reasonable requirements" with respect to such investments (Article 12:1). [3]

The history of the Havana Charter demonstrated the unwillingness of Governments to subject their investment policies — and, indeed, the whole range of their trade policies — to international rules and disciplines. The

1 See *United Nations Conference on Trade and Employment, Held at Havana, Cuba from November 21, 1947 to March 24, 1948: Final Act and Related Documents* (Lake Success, N.Y., Interim Commission for the International Trade Organization, 1948), p. 5.

2 Ibid., p. 8.

3 Ibid.

GATT itself became a permanent institution, primarily because of the unwillingness of major economic powers to adopt the Havana Charter. Since then, an informal consensus has prevailed with regard to the regulation of foreign direct investment, with sovereign discretion being virtually under no restraints, pending the adoption of an international framework on foreign direct investment as negotiated by the United Nations Commission on Transnational Corporations.

Investment issues were never a major focus in the GATT before the launching of the Uruguay Round. However, some countries have previously invoked the General Agreement in respect of some investment measures, arguing that measures pertaining to local content, export performance, etc. were trade-related and that they required detailed examination in the light of GATT articles. Efforts to extend the coverage of the General Agreement to take into account such considerations began soon after the conclusion of the Tokyo Round in 1978. A significant development in this direction was the dispute brought by the United States against Canada on the latter's administration of the Foreign Investment Review Act (FIRA) in 1982. A number of delegations, however, expressed doubts about the competence of GATT to settle that dispute, as investment legislation was not covered by the General Agreement.[4] The GATT Council finally allowed the dispute settlement Panel to proceed with its work on the presumption that the Panel would be limited in its activities and findings to issues falling within the boundaries of the General Agreement.

In its report, the FIRA Panel found that Canada's practice of allowing certain foreign direct investment under FIRA on the condition that the investors provide written undertakings to purchase goods of Canadian origin or goods from Canadian sources, was inconsistent with Article III:4 of the General Agreement. Article III:4 of the General Agreement stipulates that imported products shall be accorded treatment no less favourable than that accorded to like products of national origin in respect of requirements affecting their internal sale, purchase, transportation, distribution or use. However, the Panel also found that the undertakings to purchase Canadian goods did not prevent the importation of goods as such and were therefore not inconsistent with Article XI:1 of the General Agreement (on the prohibition of quantitative restrictions). Similarly, the Panel concluded that Canada did not act in violation of Article XVII:1 (c) of the General Agreement (which, as argued by the

4 For a record of the statements and reservations made by delegations, see General Agreement on Tariffs and Trade, *Basic Instruments and Selected Documents, 30th Supplement* (Geneva, March 1984), pp. 141-42.

United States, required that business decisions should be made only on the basis of commercial considerations), by requiring investors under FIRA to provide written undertakings that they would *export* a specified amount or proportion of their production.[5]

Argentina, in a submission before the Panel, had argued that the dispute involved two developed contracting parties and that the arguments invoked against Canada could not necessarily be invoked against developing countries, given the exception that the General Agreement accords developing countries in order to promote the establishment of a particular industry. In response to this argument, the Panel recognized that in any dispute involving less developed contracting parties, full account should be taken of the special provisions of the General Agreement relating to these countries (such as Article XVIII:C). The Panel did not examine the issues before it in the light of these provisions since the dispute only involved developed contracting parties.[6]

B. Launching of the Uruguay Round and the mandate

Even though the question of investment was informally discussed in the GATT in the early 1980s at the request of some countries which expressed concern at increases in the use of trade-related investment measures, it was during the preparatory phase of the Uruguay Round that the attempts to place investment measures on the GATT agenda gathered momentum. A proposal by the United States to the Preparatory Committee in June 1986 called upon Governments to agree that the Uruguay Round negotiations should address the means to increase discipline over government investment measures which should be controlled and reduced in the light of specific articles and overall objectives of the General Agreement. The draft text for the Ministerial Declaration entitled "Investment" suggested by the United States specified that the negotiations should address, *inter alia*, government investment measures that divert investment flows and distort trade flows, thereby reducing the contribution of trade liberalization to expanding world trade and economic growth. However, this attempt met with resistance from some developed countries and several developing countries. The mandate of the Round, as it was eventually formulated in the Punta del Este Ministerial Declaration, reflects a balance between the interests of the various parties. The aim of the negotiations on TRIMs were specified in the mandate as follows:

5 Ibid., pp. 165-166.

6 Ibid., p. 158.

> Following an examination of the operation of GATT Articles related to the trade-restrictive and distorting effects of investment measures, negotiations should elaborate, as appropriate, further provisions that may be necessary to avoid such adverse effects on trade.[7]

The Mid-Term Review Decision of the Trade Negotiations Committee, held at Montreal in December 1988, articulated this negotiating objective in a procedural fashion, in the form of a series of elements:

- Further identification of the trade restrictive and distorting effects of investment measures that are or may be covered by GATT Articles, specifying those Articles.
- Identification of other trade restrictive and distorting effects of investment measures that may not be covered adequately by existing GATT Articles but are relevant to the mandate of the Group given by the Punta del Este Ministerial Declaration.
- Development aspects that would require consideration.
- Means of avoiding the identified adverse trade effects of trade-related investment measures including, as appropriate, new provisions to be elaborated where existing GATT Articles may not cover them adequately.
- Other relevant issues, such as the modalities and implementation.[8]

The mandate specified in the Ministerial Declaration gave rise to two different interpretations in the negotiating process. On the one hand, the developing countries have argued that the aim of the negotiations is to elaborate appropriate provisions for the avoidance of adverse effects on trade caused by investment measures, and not the disciplining of investment measures *per se*. Such effects would need to be identified through a case-by-case examination of investment measures. The developed countries, on the other hand, have argued that the effects often cannot be isolated from the measures and consequently any serious attempt to tackle the trade-distorting effects of investment measures would have to deal with the measures themselves. The major divergences in the negotiations on TRIMS can be seen as emerging from these two interpretations.

---

7 "Ministerial Declaration on the Uruguay Round", in *Uruguay Round: Papers on Selected Issues* (United Nations publication, UNCTAD/ITP/10), annex 1, p. 369.

8 "Mid-term review agreements", *News of the Uruguay Round*, 27 (24 April 1989), p. 23.

C. Negotiating positions

1. The United States and Japan

The positions of the United States and Japan on TRIMS are very similar, and it is useful to discuss them together. In their submissions, these two countries have listed a number of regulatory performance requirements as having trade-distorting and inhibiting effects. A separate list of investment incentives provided by Governments has also been presented, and it has been argued that they also create distortions in trade and investment flows. The United States has argued that the General Agreement already covers trade-related investment measures and that the present negotiations should address the issue more explicitly by reviewing the relevant articles of the Agreement in depth and by elaborating additional disciplines. The United States has cited a number of articles — e.g., I, II, III, IV, XI, XV, XVII, XVIII and XXIII — as meriting detailed examination in this context. While Japan also argues for the elaboration of new disciplines on investment measures in GATT, its proposal stresses the need for the inclusion of measures imposed by both national and local governments.

Both Japan and the United States have argued that certain investment measures should be prohibited. In one of its later submissions, the United States has argued that since the mandate is to avoid adverse trade effects rather than merely compensate for them after the fact, and since certain investment measures inherently restrict or distort trade, the only way to ensure the avoidance of adverse trade effects is to prohibit inherently distorting investment measures.[9] The submission specifies that by "inherently", it means that one can reasonably presume that there will be trade distortion or restriction because the adverse trade effects are inseparable from the underlying measures. Such measures include requirements related to domestic content, domestic sourcing, manufacturing, technology transfer, local sales, foreign exchange, exports and restrictions on the production of particular goods or the use of particular technology.

Both Japan and the United States also argued for general disciplines to be imposed on all other investment measures since, according to them, certain investment measures that are not prohibited may also lead to trade distortions, especially when applied in a discriminatory manner. The United States submission cites local equity requirements and certain restrictions on remittances or access to foreign exchange as examples of these. The disciplines proposed

---

9 See MTN.GNG/NG12/W/24. See also the Japanese submission, MTN.GNG/NG12/W/20.

include the application of the principle of non-discrimination, improvement in transparency, consultation and dispute settlement provisions, etc. Both submissions propose the establishment of a TRIMs committee to oversee the implementation of the TRIMs agreement, as well as to serve as a forum for consultations on TRIMs. In relation to questions of development, the United States submission agrees that compliance with a TRIMs agreement would involve significant adjustments on the part of countries which apply such measures and of firms subject to them. The draft agreement proposed by the United States suggests a scheme for the progressive adjustment of the agreement. However, the submission stresses that the agreement should not indefinitely postpone disciplines and that there are strong arguments for brief transition periods. The argument is that if transition periods are long, important economic adjustments could be delayed and that this could disadvantage established companies in relation to new entrants.

2. *The European Community and the Nordic countries*

A second position in the negotiations on TRIMs has been that of the European Community (EC) and the Nordic countries. They have adopted a more nuanced position than that of the United States and Japan, in that they focus on investment measures that have a direct and significant restrictive impact on trade and a direct link to the existing GATT rules. In one of its later submissions, the European Community states that the negotiations should not call into question the existence of national investment policies as such, and that the objective of any discipline in the area should be the avoidance or elimination of trade distortions caused by TRIMs. Such disciplines should, to the largest extent possible, be built on existing GATT articles and principles.[10] The EC submission recognizes that in principle all investment measures can and probably will have an influence on trade, even when they are taken for reasons entirely unrelated to trade. However, as it is important that measures taken, for example, for fiscal, environmental or consumer protection purposes should not be the subject of the negotiations, it is necessary to distinguish between investment measures in general, and those that are relevant to the Uruguay Round negotiating objectives.[11] The EC considers those measures to be relevant which have a direct relation to trade measures directed at the exports and imports of a company, with the immediate objective of influencing its trade patterns. Among the 14 measures discussed in the Negotiating Group, the EC identifies eight measures as directly trade-related. They are: local

10 See MTN.GNG/NG12/W/22.

11 See MTN.GNG/NG12/W/10.

content requirements; manufacturing requirements; export-performance requirements; product-mandating requirements; trade-balancing requirements; exchange restrictions; domestic sales requirements; and manufacturing limitations concerning the components of the final product.

In the EC's view, technology transfer and licensing requirements do not qualify as relevant for the negotiations, even though they may have an impact on investors' decisions to invest or on their choice of a specific kind of investment. Similarly, licensing requirements and the tax regime applied may disadvantage the investor's competitive position, but do not appear to influence the investor's trading behaviour in a direct manner and cannot be considered as trade-related. Equity measures too, in themselves, are not directly trade-related, according to the EC position.[12] However, in a later submission, the EC has suggested that a TRIMs agreement should recognize the fact that it is perfectly possible that these measures distort or restrict trade and thus cause injury to a third party, be it the foreign investor's home country or a third country. The EC has proposed that signatories to the TRIMs agreement should, therefore, undertake a commitment to avoid causing such trade distorting and restrictive effects on trade through the use of investment measures. The EC has suggested that such a general commitment can be transposed to more operational terms by using trade policy concepts taken from Article XVIII and Article II of the General Agreement. The EC as well as the Nordic countries oppose the inclusion of right of establishment and of transfer of resources in the negotiations.[13]

In spite of the EC's insistence on directly trade-related investment measures as the proper subject of the negotiations, it does not agree with the developing country proposal that the adverse trade effects need to be determined on a case-by-case basis, and argues for generally applicable disciplines. It has cited Articles III:4, XI:1, XVII:1(c) and X:1 as requiring examination. In the EC's view, the question of exceptions can be addressed only after the provisions which prohibit or restrict the use of TRIMs have been identified by the Negotiating Group. This view implies that Article XXIII can apply to any situation leading to the nullification and impairment of benefits, such "exceptions" notwithstanding.

The Nordic countries, on the other hand, argue that the trade effects of investment measures cited in the Negotiating Group vary from TRIM to TRIM and sometimes from case to case.[14] Therefore, it would not be appropriate to

12 See MTN.GNG/NG12/W/10.

13 See MTN.GNG/NG12/W/22.

14 See MTN/GNG/NG12/W/23.

cover all TRIMs with the same disciplines. The Nordic countries suggest that both comprehensive and case-by-case approaches be used. They consider only two TRIMs — local content requirements and export-performance requirements — to be sufficiently clear-cut in their trade-distorting effects to be subject to a comprehensive discipline. In these cases, elimination should be the goal, but a gradual approach is needed so as to allow Governments and investors time to adjust. The phase-out of these measures should be based on notification, binding and elimination within an adjustment period. The Nordic countries suggest three years as the adjustment period for developed countries, five years for developing countries and 10 years for least-developed countries. For TRIMs that are not covered by the comprehensive discipline, the Nordic countries propose the application of a second level of discipline directly linked to national treatment and non-discrimination, and action on a case-by-case basis by the GATT dispute settlement mechanism. In relation to exceptions, the Nordic countries favour a strong link to the GATT Agreement, and argue that Articles XI:2, XII, XVIII:B and C, XX and XXI should be examined for their relevance when negotiating a discipline.

3. *Developing countries*

In contrast with the negotiating positions discussed above, developing countries have argued that trade-related investment measures are legitimate instruments, when applied within the broader context of economic growth and development policy, for balance-of-payments reasons and for the attainment of social and economic policy objectives consistent with the General Agreement. They have argued that the creation of a comprehensive discipline for investment measures may frustrate the above-mentioned objectives and go far beyond the original mandate of the Uruguay Round by creating an international investment regime under GATT.

The intent of the Punta del Este mandate, according to the developing countries, was to focus on the trade-restrictive and distorting effects of investment measures, and not to circumscribe the capacity of Governments to employ investment measures *per se*. Furthermore, the Ministerial Mid-term Review Decision on TRIMs not only reaffirmed the original mandate, but also stipulated that development aspects be integrated into the negotiating process. In two joint submissions, developing countries presented a list of the main development objectives for the attainment of which Governments employ investment measures.[15] They include: ensuring the most efficient and fullest contribution of investment to the national economy; enhancing and maximizing employment opportunities; facilitating restructuring under socially acceptable conditions; eliminating industrial, economic and social disadvantages of specific regions; alleviating pressures on available foreign exchange and making the most efficient use of it for the development of the external sectors; enhancing the contribution of investments to building and upgrading domestic technological capability; ensuring the most effective use of natural resources and value-added contributions to the economy; and expanding export markets.

Developing countries have also stressed that, in addition to the development objectives mentioned above, there are a number of other significant considerations that need to be taken into account in the negotiations. They have argued that such considerations create the need for Governments to use TRIMs in order to offset the trade restrictive and distorting effects of transnational corporations. For example, local content requirements may be used as a response to vertically integrated corporate enterprises holding a dominant position of market power, which might prefer to source components and parts from parent companies or foreign sources even if comparable inputs are locally available. Manufacturing requirements may be used by host country Governments to avoid abusive pricing practices by transnational corporations or to protect local firms from predatory practices. Domestic sales requirements are often necessary to counteract the corporate entities' refusal to deal or unfair cartel pricing. Export-performance requirements are often a means for host country Governments to curb export prohibitions at the enterprise level and also to ensure quality products for competition in world markets.

The developing country submissions have also contested the applicability of GATT articles in relation to questions of investment. They argue that the General Agreement is designed to deal with international trade in goods, as they cross international frontiers and, as TRIMs are not border measures, the Agreement does not apply to them. In so far as investment measures imposed at the point of production deal with acts of exportation or importation, establishing the link between border measures and TRIMs will involve complex difficulties. To the extent that investment measures have an adverse effect on trade, such effect would need to be demonstrated on a case-by-case basis. The developing countries also pointed out that the existing provisions in the

15 See joint submission by 11 developing countries (Argentina, Brazil, Cameroon, China, Colombia, Cuba, Egypt, India, United Republic of Tanzania and Yugoslavia), MTN/GNG/NG12/W/25; and Draft Declaration on TRIMs submitted by Bangladesh, Brazil, Colombia, Cuba, Egypt, India, Kenya, Nigeria, Pakistan, Peru, United Republic of Tanzania and Zimbabwe, MTN/GNG/NG12/W/26.

General Agreement for remedies in the event of nullification and/or impairment of benefits would be sufficient to deal with the alleged adverse effects of some of the investment measures cited in the Negotiating Group.

Many developing countries also questioned the applicability of individual articles of the General Agreement to TRIMs. Singapore and India have argued that Article I deals with discriminatory trade measures, and not with discriminatory effects.[16] Furthermore, Article I deals with border measures and not with production measures. Article II is concerned with whether a Government imposes additional charges on imports. The Singapore submission argued that if a TRIM increases the cost of importing, it is not a violation of this Article. Article III deals with discrimination between imported and domestic goods, and as such does not apply to a manufacturing requirement which is a production measure, which falls outside the scope of the General Agreement. The Indian submission stated that Article VI does not apply to TRIMs, as there is no evidence to establish a causal relationship between export performance measures and dumping. If, in certain circumstances, they lead to dumping of exports, the existing provisions in the Agreement against dumping would seem to suffice. Article XI deals with the importation of products and not those affecting imported products, dealt with in Article III. Hence, India argues, it does not apply to performance requirements. Furthermore, in applying this article in relation to investment measures, full consideration would need to be given to the provisions in the General Agreement that allow developing countries to maintain import restrictions for balance-of-payments reasons. Article XVI concerns subsidies and its applicability to TRIMs has also been questioned by developing countries, arguing that if contracting parties are of the view that the products are being subsidized the existing remedies would suffice. The developing countries also stressed the provisions in Article XVIII which recognizes that it may be necessary for developing countries, in order to implement programmes and policies for economic development, to take protective or other measures affecting imports and that such measures are justified in so far as they facilitate the attainment of the objectives of the General Agreement.

In short, developing countries have argued that the prohibition of certain TRIMs would be a transgression of the limits of the Punta del Este mandate, that it will frustrate the development objectives of developing countries and the efficient use of investment therein and create an international regime with rights for investors and without any accompanying obligations for them.

---

16 See the statement by Singapore, MTN.GNG/NG12/W/17, and the submission by India, MTN.GNG/NG12/W/18.

D. Pre-Brussels developments

Although the Negotiating Group on TRIMs considered a number of draft texts, including some proposed by the Chairperson of the Group, basic divergences continued to persist among negotiating partners concerning several fundamental aspects of a possible TRIMs agreement. Four areas, where basic divergences were perceived to persist, were identified in the document submitted to the Ministers at the Brussels meeting of the Trade Negotiations Committee in December 1990. [17] They concerned the coverage of the agreement, the level of discipline to be imposed, the treatment of developing countries in the agreement and the treatment of restrictive business practices.

In relation to *coverage*, there were differences of view regarding whether a TRIMs agreement should cover measures imposed only when an investment is made, or should also include measures applied to established firms and industries. The definition of investment measures proposed by the United States includes measures applied by a contracting party as a condition for the continued operation of a company, thereby extending the coverage of the agreement to measures applied to established firms or companies. Another aspect of the question of coverage concerns TRIMs that are enforceable through a government offering or withdrawal of advantages, and particularly subsidies. The EC has argued that, as government incentives (including subsidies), are being discussed in the Negotiating Group on subsidies, such incentives should not be the subject of the current negotiations on TRIMs. However, an incentive does not eliminate the trade-distorting effect of a performance requirement attached as a condition to it. The United States submission, while specifying that the draft agreement proposed by them does not establish disciplines on investment incentives *per se,* includes under investment measures those applied by a contracting party as a condition for the receipt of an incentive or services necessary for the conduct of business.

A second major issue on which negotiating positions have shown basic divergence is that of the *level of discipline* to be imposed by an agreement on TRIMs. The United States and Japan have argued for a two-tier discipline, involving the prohibition of those TRIMs that are seen as inherently trade-restricting and distorting in their effect, and a general discipline applicable to all TRIMs that are not prohibited by the agreement. They have argued that certain TRIMs (such as local content requirements) have already been prohibited by the General Agreement under Articles III and XI, and that new provisions for the prohibition of TRIMs (such as export-performance require-

17 See MTN.TNC/W/35/Rev. 1. See also section E below.

ments) need to be made. Developing countries, on the other hand, have argued that the prohibition of TRIMs will be a transgression of the mandate of the negotiations, and that the trade-distorting effects of TRIMs, if any, should be examined on a case-by-case basis. They have also stated that the prohibition of TRIMs would adversely affect the efficient use of investment in the broader context of development and balance-of-payments policies, and frustrate the development objectives of developing countries.

Divergences also exist in relation to the *treatment of developing countries* in the agreement. The Ministerial Mid-term Review Decision had mentioned development aspects among the elements to be integrated into the negotiating process. Developing countries, in their joint draft agreement, have sought recognition for the use of investment measures as legitimate instruments, when used by Governments in the context of economic growth and development policy. They have argued that the contracting parties should be allowed to employ investment measures in the context of their programmes and policies to promote socio-economic growth and development. Developed countries, on the other hand, have argued for the same disciplines to be applicable to all participants, irrespective of their stage of development. The United States and Japan have suggested schemes for adjusting to an agreement progressively, with different transition periods for developed, developing and least-developed countries. The EC has also proposed the application of special transition periods for developing countries, except those that have reached a high level of international competitiveness.

Marked differences also exist in relation to the *treatment of restrictive business practices* of corporate entities in the agreement. As noted above, developing countries have argued that TRIMs are often applied by developing countries in order to counteract such trade-restrictive practices and to prevent the abuse of a dominant position of market power by corporate entities. They have argued that restrictive business practices can lead to significant welfare losses to developing countries and that disciplining of investment measures without any corresponding discipline on restrictive business practices will aggravate the position of developing countries. They have sought recognition in the agreement of the need for Governments to use investment measures in order to offset such practices. However, developed countries have resisted proposals to this effect.

As a result of these basic divergences of negotiating positions in the TRIMs Group, no draft could be formulated, even with square-brackets, that could commonly be accepted as a basis for negotiations.

E. Brussels and after

The meeting of the Trade Negotiations Committee of the Uruguay Round at the Ministerial level in Brussels from 3 to 7 December 1990 had been anticipated by the Director-General of GATT, at the meeting of the Trade Negotiations Group in Geneva on 26 November 1990, to be the final political meeting of the Uruguay Round. Earlier, it had been generally expected that this meeting would mark the culmination of the negotiating process, the most complex and ambitious Round of trade negotiations ever undertaken under the aegis of GATT. However, the document that was presented before the Ministers [18] contained 391 pages, with heavily square-bracketed texts in several areas and no text at all in a few of the others. TRIMs was an area in which no draft agreement was presented before the Ministers. There was only an enumeration of major areas of disagreement among trading partners in this area, i.e., coverage, level of discipline, developing countries and restrictive business practices. As a result of sustained differences between the European Community and the United States on an agreement on agriculture, the negotiations broke down on 6 December 1990.

The Uruguay Round negotiations were subsequently resumed on 21 February 1991. Under the new negotiating structure, TRIMs has been merged with other rule-making issues as one group, and only some technical discussions have been carried out since the resumption of the negotiations in February with a view to elaborating a workable "effects test" that would be useful in determining the scope and definition of TRIMs. In his report to the Chairperson of the Group of Negotiations on Goods, the Chairperson of the new Negotiating Group on Rule-Making and TRIMs indicated that an intensification of the negotiations could be initiated after the summer break, based on a detailed consideration of a list of issues, which includes: coverage of the agreement; disciplines; treatment of developing countries; transition periods; restrictive business practices; and other issues. He expected that such a discussion would greatly assist him in the presentation, at the appropriate time, of a draft text which could form the basis of further negotiations on this subject. The new Negotiating Group on Rule-Making and TRIMs has decided to meet again by the end of September 1991.

18 See MTN.TNC/W/35/Rev. 1.

Appendix B

A simple model of "production-shifting" in an oligopolistic global industry with increasing returns to scale [1]

In this model, a large number of potential investment sites is scattered among various countries capable of producing a good for world markets at approximately comparable costs if a transnational investor locates an indivisible facility within their borders. The scale of production is such that only a few of the countries will be hosts to a facility. (Besides the automotive, computer fabrication and petrochemical industries examined below one might want to include, for example, copper and petroleum refineries, agrochemical and pharmaceutical plants, pulp and paper mills and other wood products.)

Using partial equilibrium analysis, the international price for the product is represented as an inverse demand curve:

$$P = D(Q) \tag{1}$$

where Q is the total production of the good and supply from all other firms (except the transnational corporation in question) is taken as fixed.

Let p be the local supply price for the good (generally less than P), with an upward sloping supply curve:

$$p = S(q) \tag{2}$$

where q is the production from the country in question.

1 This model is an adaptation of one developed by Paul Krugman, "New trade theory and the less developed countries", in Guillermo Calvo, ed., *Debt, Stabilization, and Development* (Cambridge, Mass., B. Blackwell for WIDER, 1989). The adaptation was facilitated by Martin Richardson.

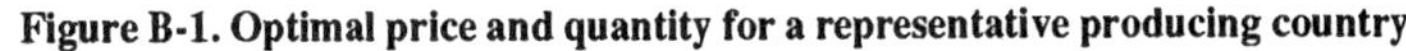

Figure B-1. Optimal price and quantity for a representative producing country

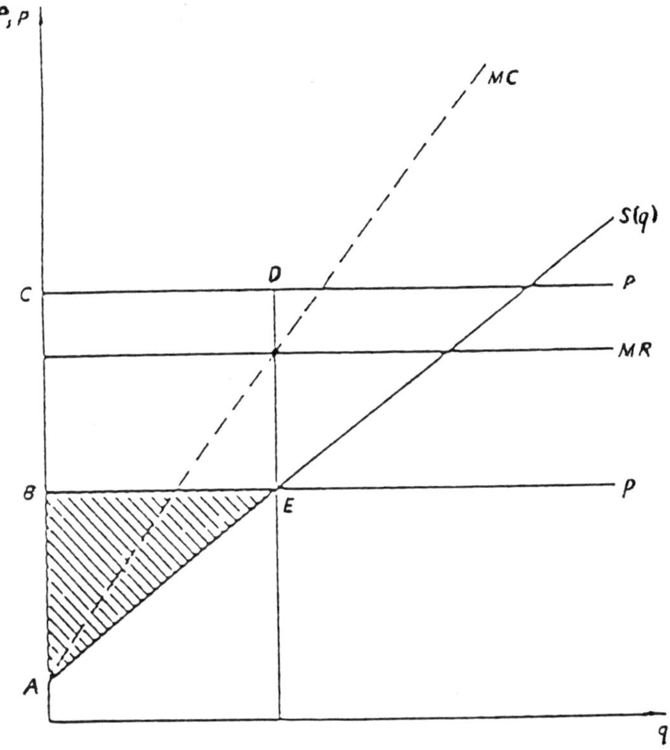

Source: Adapted from Paul Krugman, "New trade theory and the less developed countries", in Guillermo Calvo, ed., *Debt, Stabilization, and Development* (Cambridge, Mass., B. Blackwell for WIDER, 1989).

The transnational corporation will calculate the marginal cost of output to be the local supply price plus the effect of additional purchases in increasing the price of the intramarginal inputs:

$$MC = p + q\,(\partial p / \partial q) \tag{3}$$

The transnational firm will derive the marginal revenue from output sales by subtracting the effect of increased sales on intramarginal units from the world price:

$$MR = P + q\,(\partial P / \partial Q) \tag{4}$$

In equilibrium, marginal revenue is equal to marginal cost:

$$MR = MC \tag{5}$$

which means the transnational firm collects a rent from its monopoly and monopsony power equal to the wedge between world and local prices:

$$P - p = q\,(\partial p / \partial q - \partial P / \partial Q) \tag{6}$$

In this representation, the number of plants is fixed. At any given volume and price, there are numerous equilibria with different trade flows but identical overall welfare. The differences between the equilibria do matter to the individual countries, however, since countries that have production facilities gain in relation to those that do not.

Figure B-1 illustrates the situation of any one country which might be a site for a production facility, using equations (1) through (5).

For simplification, the world price P and the marginal revenue are sketched as horizontal. The local supply curve is P = S(q), with the marginal cost curve drawn to the left.

In equilibrium, the area BCDE depicts the potential rent to the transnational firm at any given site. The shaded area ABE represents a producer surplus that the country captures if a plant is located within its borders. The producer surplus in this model takes the form of higher earnings for those parts of the population associated with the project, that is, sub-marginal workers and suppliers gain more if the country hosts the project than if it does not. Thus, which countries capture the production facilities within their borders is important for national welfare.

This model reveals hazards as well as opportunities if countries follow their own individual self-interests.

On the one hand, an activist Government can pursue not only the producer surplus (ABE) but also a large portion of the transnational corporation's rent (say, by levying a lump-sum tax for right of establishment). The transnational corporation would be willing to pay up to the amount (BCDE) if it had no alternatives.

On the other hand, an activist Government should be willing to grant a subsidy to ensure that it gets a facility that matches (and slightly exceeds) the subsidy offered by any other country. The result could be a subsidy war which not only remits all of (BCDE) to the transnational corporation but squanders the producer surplus (ABE) as well.

The analysis illustrates the need for policy activism on the part of host countries that want to advance, or defend, their national interests, but also reveals the drawbacks if all countries adopt an activist stance.

Appendix C

The effects of alternative forms of public interventions on the profitability of investors who choose a target locale [1]

There have been impressive advances in understanding the comparability between fiscal and trade incentives, and combining both in a single measure that captures the net effect of public policies designed to raise the profitability of investors who choose a particular locale for their operations. What is needed is to calculate the effect on corporate profitability of policies directed at factor markets (like tax holidays, special rates for depreciation and amortization, cash grants, subsidized loans and employment allowances), as well as policies directed at goods markets (like trade restrictions). The most sophisticated synthesis thus far has been carried out by Stephen Guisinger. [2]

Beginning on the fiscal side, recent analysis has moved beyond an examination of tax rates to examine all fiscal and monetary instruments which affect the profitability of corporate operations. Douglas Yuill and Kevin Allen, for example, converted fiscal incentives in the European Community into "cash grant equivalents" which together would equal a hypothetical cash payment rational investors would accept in the first year of a project in place of fiscal incentives which the laws of the various European Community States entitled them to receive. [3] Gary Hufbauer combined both cash and non-cash incentives (e.g., tax holidays) into a measure called the "rental cost of capital". [4] Mervyn A. King and Don Fullerton have assimilated the effects of all

1 This analysis is derived from Stephen Guisinger, "Total protection: a new measure of the impact of government interventions on investment profitability", *Journal of International Business Studies*, vol. 20 (Summer 1989), pp. 280-295.

2 Ibid.

3 Douglas Yuill and Kevin Allen, *European Regional Incentives* (Glasgow, Centre for the Study of Public Policy, University of Strathclyde, 1986).

4 Gary Clyde Hufbauer, "The taxation of export profits", *National Tax Journal*, 28 (1975).

Figure C-1. Isoreturn curve: combinations of protection and cash grants that yield a 15 per cent rate of return a/

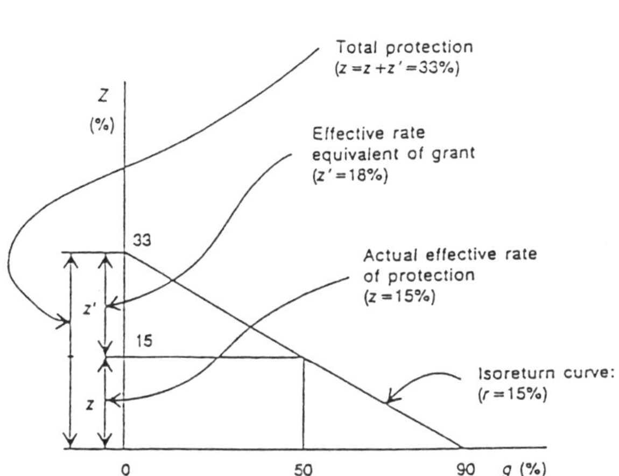

Source: Stephen Guisinger, "Total protection: A new measure of the impact of government interventions on investment profitability", *Journal of International Business Studies*, 20 (Summer 1989), pp. 280-295.

Note: g = grant.
z = protection.

a/ The conditions for this illustration are: a corporate tax rate of 40 per cent, a share of value-added at free trade going to equity and to depreciation of 20 per cent (each), a tariff on capital good imports of 10 per cent, an annuitized present value of accelerated depreciation allowances of 2 per cent of value-added, an investor's discount rate of 10 per cent and a capital-output ratio at world prices of 2.

fiscal policies into a single "marginal effective rate of taxation".[5] All of these studies, however, do not include the impact of trade policies on the returns from a given project.

To fill this gap, Bela Belassa took the effective rate of protection (the increase in a sector's value-added attributable to trade restrictions) and added to it an estimate of fiscal incentives (above), calling this the "effective rate of subsidy".[6] Christopher Findlay and Ross Garnaut used the term "effective rate

5 Mervyn A. King and Don Fullerton, *The Taxation of Income from Capital* (Chicago, The University of Chicago Press, 1984).

6 Bela Belassa *et al.*, *Development Strategies in Semi-Industrial Economies* (Baltimore, Johns Hopkins University Press, 1982).

of assistance" in a similar approach as part of their study of trade and non-trade forms of public assistance in Australia.[7]

Guisinger refined the Belassa-Findlay-Garnaut approach by focusing on how the effective rate of protection supports one factor of production, the profitability of capital.[8] He ended up with a model that shows how the effective rate of protection, the cash-grant equivalent of government subsidies and the decreases in the rental cost of capital (tax holidays, for example) relate to the investor's after-tax rate of return.

Using plausible (but merely illustrative) conditions, figure C-1 demonstrates how effective rates of protection and cash grants can be combined to yield a 15 per cent rate of return on a given project (a similar relationship can be established to illustrate substitution possibilities between effective protection and the rental cost of capital).

7 Christopher Findlay and Ross Garnaut, *The Political Economy of Manufacturing Protection: Experiences of ASEAN and Australia* (Sydney, Allen and Unwin, 1986).

8 Guisinger, "Total protection", op. cit.

SELECT LIST OF PUBLICATIONS

A. United Nations Conference on Trade and Development

Uruguay Round: Papers on Selected Issues, UNCTAD/ITP/10.

Uruguay Round: Further Papers on Selected Issues, UNCTAD/ITP/42.

Technology, Trade Policy and the Uruguay Round, UNCTAD/ITP/23.

Trade in Services: Selected Issues, UNCTAD/ITP/26.

Services and Development Potential: The Indian Context, UNCTAD/ITP/22.

Services in Asia and the Pacific, vol. I, UNCTAD/ITP/51.

Services in Asia and the Pacific, vol. II, UNCTAD/ITP/51 vol. II.

Mexico: Una Economia de Servicios, UNCTAD/ITP/58.

Trade and Development Report 1988, 1989, 1990, 1991.

B. United Nations Centre on Transnational Corporations

1. Individual studies

World Investment Report 1991: The Triad in Foreign Direct Investment. 108 p. Sales No. E.91.II.A.12. $25.

Transnational Corporations in South Africa: A List of Companies with Investments and Disinvestments. 282 p. Sales No. E.91.II.A.9. $22.

University Curriculum on Transnational Corporations:
Vol. I *Economic Development*. 188 p. Sales No. E.91.II.A.5. $20.
Vol. II *International Business*. 156 p. Sales No. E.91.II.A.6. $20.
Vol. III *International Law*. 180 p. Sales No. E.91.II.A.7. $20.
The Set: Sales No. E.91.II.A.8. $50.

Directory of the World's Largest Service Companies: Series I. 834 p. ISSN 1014-8507. $295 ($95 to public/academic libraries). (Joint publication, UNCTC/Moody's Investors Service.)

The Challenge of Free Economic Zones in Central and Eastern Europe. 444 p. Sales No. E.90.II.A.27. $75.

Accountancy Development in Africa: Challenge of the 1990s. 206 p. Sales No. E.91.II.A.2. $25. (Also available in French.)

Transnational Banks and the International Debt Crisis. 157 p. Sales No. E.90.II.A.19. $22.50.

Transborder Data Flows and Mexico: A Technical Paper. 194 p. Sales No. E.90.II.A.17. $27.50.

Debt Equity Conversions: A Guide For Decision-Makers. 150 p. Sales No. E.90.II.A.22. $27.50.

Transnational Corporations and Manufacturing Exports from Developing Countries. 124 p. Sales No. E.90.II.A.21. $25.

Transnational Corporations in the Transfer of New and Emerging Technologies to Developing Countries. 141 p. Sales No. E.90.II.A.20. $27.50.

Transnational Corporations, Services, and the Uruguay Round. 252 p. Sales No. E.90.II.A.11. $28.50.

The Uruguay Round: Services in the World Economy, 220 p., ISBN 0-8213-1374-6. $13.95. (Joint publication, UNCTC/World Bank.)

Transnational Corporations in the Plastics Industry. 167 p. Sales No. E.90.II.A.1. $20.

2. Serial publications

UNCTC Current Studies, Series A

No. 12 *New Approaches to Best-practice Manufacturing: The Role of Transnational Corporations and Implications for Developing Countries.* 76 p. Sales No. E.90.II.A.13. $12.50.

No. 13 *Key Concepts in International Investment Arrangements and Their Relevance to Negotiations on International Transactions in Services.* 66 p. Sales No. E.90.II.A.3. $9.

No. 14 *The Role of Free Economic Zones in the USSR and Eastern Europe.* 84 p. Sales No. E.90.II.A.5. $10.

No. 15 *Economic Integration and Transnational Corporations in the 1990s: Europe 1992, North America and Developing Countries.* 52 p. Sales No. E.90.II.A.14. $12.50.

No. 16 *The New Code Environment.* 54 p. Sales No. E.90.II.A.7. $7.50.

No. 19 *New Issues in the Uruguay Round of Multilateral Trade Negotiations.* 52 p. Sales No. E.90.II.A.15. $12.50.

No. 20 *Foreign Direct Investment, Debt and Home Country Policies.* 50 p. Sales No. E.90.II.A.16. $12.

UNCTC Advisory Studies, Series B

No. 5 *Negotiating International Hotel Chain Management Agreements.* 60 p. Sales No. E.90.II.A.8. $9.

No. 6 *Curricula for Accounting Education for East-West Joint Ventures in Centrally Planned Economies.* 86 p. Sales No. E.90.II.A.2. $10.

No. 7 *Joint Venture Accounting in the USSR: Direction for Change.* 46 p. Sales No. E.90.II.A.26. $12.

International Accounting and Reporting Issues:

1984 Review. 122 p. Sales No. E.85.II.A.2. $13.50.
1985 Review. 141 p. Sales No. E.85.II.A.13. $15.
1986 Review. 158 p: Sales No. E.86.II.A.16. $15.
1987 Review. 140 p. Sales No. E.88.II.A.8. $17.
(Also published by Graham & Trotman, London/Dordrecht/Boston. $65).
1988 Review. 95 p. Sales No. E.88.II.A.3. $12.
*1989 Review.*152 p. Sales No.E.90.II.A.4. $12.
1990 Review. 254 p. Sales No. E.91.II.A.3. $25.

National Legislation and Regulations Relating to Transnational Corporations:

Vol. I (Part One)	302 p. Sales No. E.78.II.A.3. $16.
Vol. I (Part Two — Supplement)	114 p. Sales No. E.80.II.A.5. $9.
Vol. II	338 p. Sales No. E.83.II.A.7. $33.
Vol. III	345 p. Sales No. E.83.II.A.15. $33.
Vol. IV	241 p. Sales No. E.85.II.A.14. $23.
Vol. V	246 p. Sales No. E.86.II.A.3. $23.
Vol. VI	322 p. Sales No. E.87.II.A.6. $45.
Vol. VII	320 p. Sales No. E.89.II.A.9. $36.

Transnational Corporations in South Africa and Namibia: United Nations Public Hearings:

Vol. I *Reports of the Panel of Eminent Persons and of the Secretary-General.* 242 p. Sales No. E.86.II.A.6. $65.

Vol. II * *Verbatim Records.* 300 p. Sales No. E.86.II.A.7.

Vol. III *Statements and Submissions*. 518 p. Sales No. E.86.II.A.8. $54.
Vol. IV * *Policy Instruments and Statements*. 444 p. Sales No. E.86.II.A.9.
Four-volume set — $200.
* May not be purchased separately.

Transnational Corporations in South Africa: Second United Nations Public Hearings, 1989

Vol. I *Report of the Panel of Eminent Persons, Background Documentation*. 162 p. Sales No. E.90.II.A.6. $19.
Vol. II *Statements and Submission*. 209 p. Sales No. E.90.II.A.20. $21.

Transnational Corporations (formerly ***The CTC Reporter***). Published three times a year. Individual issues $10. Annual subscription, which includes three issues and the report of the annual meetings of the Commission on Transnational Corporations — $30.

Transnationals, a quarterly newsletter, is available free of charge.

United Nations publications may be obtained from bookstores and distributors throughout the world. Please consult your bookstore or write to:

United Nations Publications

Sales Section	OR	Sales Section
Room DC2-0853		United Nations Office at Geneva
United Nations Secretariat		Palais des Nations
New York, N.Y. 10017		CH-1211 Geneva 10
U.S.A.		Switzerland

All prices are quoted in United States dollars.

For further information on the work of the Centre, please address inquiries to:

United Nations Centre on Transnational Corporations
Room DC2-1322
United Nations
New York, N.Y. 10017, U.S.A.

Telephone: (212) 963-3176
Telefax: (212) 963-3062
Telex: UNCTNC 661062

QUESTIONNAIRE

The Impact of Trade-related Investment Measures on Trade and Development: Theory, Evidence and Policy Implications
(ST/CTC/120)

In order to improve the quality and relevance of the work of the United Nations Centre on Transnational Corporations (UNCTC), it would be useful to receive the views of readers on this and other similar publications. It would therefore be greatly appreciated if you could complete the following questionnaire and return it to:

Readership Survey
Centre on Transnational Corporations
United Nations, Room DC2-1212
New York, N.Y. 10017, USA

1. Name and address of respondent (optional):

____

____

____

2. Which of the following best describes your area of work?

Government	☐	Public enterprise	☐
Private enterprise	☐	Academic or research institution	☐
International organization	☐	Media	☐
Non-profit organization	☐	Other (specify) ______________	

3. In which country do you work? ______________________

4. What is your assessment of the contents of this publication?

Excellent	☐	Adequate	☐
Good	☐	Poor	☐

5. How useful is this publication to your work?

   Very useful ☐ Of some use ☐ Irrelevant ☐

6. Please indicate the three things you liked best about this publication:

   ____

   ____

   ____

7. Please indicate the three things you liked least about this publication:

   ____

   ____

   ____

8. If you have read more than the present UNCTC publication, what is your overall assessment of them?

   Consistently good ☐ Usually good, but with some exceptions ☐

   Generally mediocre ☐ Poor ☐

9. On the average, how useful are these publications to you in your work?

   Very useful ☐ Of some use ☐ Irrelevant ☐

10. Are you a regular recipient of ***Transnational Corporations*** (formerly ***The CTC Reporter***), the Centre's tri-annual publication which reports on the Centre's and related work?

    Yes ☐ No ☐

    If not, please check here if you would like to receive a sample copy sent to the name and address you have given above ☐

How to obtain United Nations publications

For more information on how to obtain United Nations publications, or to receive a copy of our most recent catalogue, please write to:

United Nations Publications
United Nations
Room DC2-0853
New York, New York 10017
Fax No. (212) 963-4116, *or:*

United Nations Publications
Sales Section
Palais des Nations
1211 Geneva 10
Switzerland

Litho in United Nations, New York
41174–December 1991–4,850
ISBN 92-1-104377-8

United Nations publication
Sales No. E.91.II.A.19
ST/CTC/120